STARGATE ATLANTIS ™

THE OFFICIAL COMPANION

SEASON 4

STARGATE: ATLANTIS: THE OFFICIAL COMPANION SEASON 4

ISBN: 9781845767143

Published by
Titan Books
A division of
Titan Publishing Group Ltd
144 Southwark Street
London
SE1 0UP

First edition October 2008
2 4 6 8 10 9 7 5 3 1

DEDICATION

In memory of Don S. Davis, beloved elder statesman of the entire Stargate universe.

ACKNOWLEDGEMENTS

David Hewlett rocks in a sci-fi geek way for writing his great Foreword despite being in the midst of his wedding celebrations — and particularly for tracking me down via the Internet to make sure I got it! As always, massive thanks to the producers and writers of Stargate: Atlantis, who are always so generous with their time — Joe Mallozzi, Paul Mullie, Brad Wright, Robert C. Cooper, John Lenic, Martin Gero, Carl Binder, Alan McCullough, Andy Mikita, Will Waring. Thanks to Alex Levine and Lawren Bancroft-Wilson for fielding my calls. Thanks to Mark Savela for providing such beautiful imagery (those four drinks will come your way soon, I promise). Big, big thanks to everyone else who was interviewed for the book — and especially to Amanda Tapping and Martin Wood for being such pros despite working flat-out on their own show. As always this book could not have happened without the inimitable Brigitte Prochaska, whose almost superhuman ability to get things done continues to impress me (not to mention fill me with relief). Jo Boylett has done another fantastic job of editing (phew). Last but not least, thanks once again to Karol Mora at MGM, whom I will be plying with single malt in gratitude. Thanks, one and all!

Titan Books would like to thank all the *Stargate: Atlantis* cast and crew, in particular Paul Mullie and Joseph Mallozzi, David Hewlett for the Foreword, and Mark Savela for the vfx images. And thanks, as always, to Karol Mora at MGM.

STARGATE ATLANTIS™

THE OFFICIAL COMPANION

SEASON 4   SHARON GOSLING

STARGATE: ATLANTIS DEVELOPED FOR TELEVISION BY
BRAD WRIGHT AND ROBERT C. COOPER

TITAN BOOKS

CONTENTS

FOREWORD

Thiese stars and planets, these distant constellations — I have dreamt of them all since I was a child. I have met these foes before in nightmares. In daydreams I have defeated them. I have saved this world a million times and countless others along the way. In kindergarten I claimed to have been stranded here by aliens. I was piloting my first planet-saving robot by the time I was five. I was working on my first "sonic screwdriver" before I was ten. I

have been preparing for this existence all my life. *Stargate: Atlantis* may not be "real", I may not possess the skills and intelligence necessary to do what my friend Dr Rodney McKay has done, but I still feel like I've been here before. In science fiction I have found my home.

We are different, you and I. For us, no genre holds more promise than science fiction. Through its all-seeing eye we gaze longingly at things to come. To those of us who live under its spell, science fiction is longing. We long for the keys to Doctor Who's TARDIS. We long for epic struggles towards our destiny on distant desert planets, be they inhabited by *Dune*'s giant worms or the tiny droid-scavenging marauders of *Star Wars*. We long to be lost in *Neuromancer* skies that are "the color of a television tuned to a dead channel". We long to question whether the promise of "a better life in the off-world colonies" can compare with Replicant hunting on *Blade Runner*'s rainy, destroyed Earth. Only we truly feel the cold alloy of the weapons in our sweaty hands as we engage the enemy in space combat. Only we feel the very fabric of our being torn apart when we step through that event horizon. We envy the solitary sadness of a lone traveler in time and space because he holds the keys to the universe. We discuss and debate the minutiae of worlds we've never been to and lands that will never be. To us the Internet is another vast kingdom to conquer, another terrifying space in which to lose ourselves. Our computers are both old friends and new enemies laying in wait (because we, of all people, know how technology will soon evolve and turn on us). We look at the world, hoping to catch a glimpse of something that tells us that we're not alone. We struggle against assimilation. We are always ready for a stirring in the Force, or a glitch in the Matrix. Something sets us apart. It's not that we're better than the rest of the population — they have wisely given themselves up to the "real" world. It's just that we have designs on an infinite array of other worlds. It's doubtful that any of us have innate super-powers or skills that we will be called upon to summon up at a time of great peril. But we long for it none the less.

Science fiction lead me to a love affair with film and television. I am now honored to have a hand in creating it myself. A few *SG-1* episodes and five seasons of *Stargate: Atlantis* have given Dr Rodney McKay and I more fun and adventure than anyone could imagine. Every day is a new beginning, every episode its own unique challenge. More than this, *Atlantis* has given us both friends for life. I may have dreamt of this since before I can remember, but *Atlantis* has exceeded all my dreams. Science fiction is about dreaming, and *Stargate* has made them all come true. I can only hope that it does the same for you.

DAVID HEWLETT
Vancouver, June 2008

NEW HORIZONS BECKON

INTO SEASON 4

> "Dead and buried and turned to dust a long, long time ago, along with everyone you ever knew. There's no way of knowing what the state of human civilization is — whether it even still exists." — McKay

N
o season of a television show ever runs completely smoothly — it's a huge machine with many cogs, some of which are bound to need maintenance now and then — but *Stargate: Atlantis*'s fourth season held more challenges for the producers than most. For a start, co-creator Brad Wright, who had been running the show since its launch in 2004, had finally decided that he needed a break. It was well deserved — having also launched and run *Stargate SG-1* way back in 1997, Wright had been working on the franchise for a decade.

Into his place stepped the writing team of Joseph Mallozzi and Paul Mullie. The pair had been part of the *Stargate* universe for a very long time, having first joined the *SG-1* writing and producing team for that show's fourth season. Since the two shows were produced side by side between 2004 and 2006, Mallozzi and Mullie were also intimately acquainted with the workings of *Stargate: Atlantis*, and their appointment as show runners made the transition run as smoothly as possible under the circumstances. In fact, they had been preparing for the role for some time.

"Every year Brad would say, 'I'm exhausted, I can't do this for another year,'" laughs Mallozzi, "and then he would come back for another year… And come back for another year!"

"Finally he decided he didn't want to do that any more," Mullie explains. "He was tired and he needed a break, and he wanted to do the *Stargate SG-1* movies. And basically, we were just there. We were next in line, because we had been semi-show running *Stargate SG-1*. We had been running our own episodes, and about half the episodes with Robert [Cooper]."

"It's weird not being a show runner on a series you created," Wright acknowledges. "But Paul and Joe have been around for so long, and Martin and Carl have of course been with the show from the beginning, and Robert and I were in the room with them, helping them break stories at the beginning. So it didn't feel all that different, in many ways. It just meant that at the end of the day, my life was going to be easier than theirs," he chuckles. "But the trust factor, the belief in what they were going to do, was always there."

The pair's experience, both of the *Stargate* franchise and of producing, was an ideal primer for taking over the running of *Stargate: Atlantis*. Even so, show running a series is very different to producing individual or even numerous episodes of the same show.

"The day-to-day stuff of the show is no different — doing the meetings and the prep and so on," observes Mullie. "But there was a whole layer that goes on top of that that we had never had to deal with before."

Despite this added layer of duties to fulfil, Mallozzi and Mullie zealously threw themselves into pre-production on season four. For the writer/producers who had previously worked under Brad Wright, including Martin Gero and Carl Binder, the change in who was ultimately calling the shots in the writers' room seemed perfectly natural — and pretty unobtrusive.

"I've been working with Joe and Paul since the beginning," explains Gero. "It's a very small office here. We all have lunch together every day, we all read each other's scripts, we all watch each other's cuts. So although Joe and Paul had written fewer *Atlantis* episodes than *SG-1* episodes, they were still a very present and important creative force behind the show. On the outside it might have seemed like a big power change, but for us it was a very organic thing. For Carl and I, who have been working on the show since season one, it was a really seamless transition. Not to take away anything from Brad and Rob — we're friends — but when I started they were my bosses! With Joe and Paul taking over, it felt like we were on a more equal footing. It was a bunch of peers running the show, and they have final say over it. I think they did a great job — I think season four is our best season so far."

With Mallozzi and Mullie came several other names and faces that transferred from *Stargate SG-1* to *Stargate: Atlantis*. One was writer Alan McCullough, who would be writing for the series for the first time. Another was *Stargate SG-1* producer and production manager John Lenic, who had his own learning curve to navigate as he got used to managing *Stargate: Atlantis*.

Above: Ronon Dex (Jason Momoa) discovers he is not alone in the universe — unfortunately.

"Joe and Paul and I have a great working relationship," Lenic explains. "We worked on *SG-1* after Brad and Robert left, and I came over to *Atlantis* with them. But as much as I'd read every *Stargate: Atlantis* script from season one onwards, it really is a change of show. Most of *Atlantis* takes place in space, whereas *SG-1*, every episode had the element of being on location in the forest or something like that. So it was different, getting used to being on the stage most of the time."

New show runners in a writers' room can often mean a change of tone or direction for the series overall. They may wish to explore new themes, different aspects of a character or want to introduce new plot threads to investigate. For Mallozzi and Mullie, their established involvement in the series and long preparation for becoming show runners allowed them to formulate a rough idea for the season before pre-production even began.

"I don't know about change," ponders Mallozzi, "but the fact that we knew early enough allowed us to come up with a game plan. We wanted to sit down with the actors and say, 'Look, this is what we have in store, this is what we're thinking in regards to your characters.' We had a little more time, so we wanted to redress an

Below: John Sheppard (Joe Flanigan) contemplates his past.

imbalance in terms of the stories we were telling. There was a lot of McKay focus in two and three. David is wonderful so it was always easy to go there, but you do so much McKay at the expense of the other characters. We wanted to do a story for Teyla, a story for Ronon, a story for McKay, a story for Sheppard. And that's what we did to start off last season. In the first half, all the characters had a story and then we had a nice mix of team-oriented stories as well."

In thinking about where they wanted to take the show, Mullie and Mallozzi also made several big decisions that involved finishing certain plotlines. One concerned an enemy which had been growing in power for two seasons, but which the writers felt were on the wane.

"We thought at the time that the Asurans were played out," Mallozzi states. "We wanted to deal with them in a big way, so we kicked off the Wraith-Replicator war and finished the Replicator threat in 'Be All My Sins Remember'd'. There was also the Beckett thing."

"Yeah," adds Mullie, "we knew we wanted to bring him back, but we

Above: Sheppard does his bit for intergalactic relations.

didn't really know when or how. We knew we wanted to do a Teyla story and we knew we wanted to destroy the Replicators. That was pretty much it. We had plenty of time in advance to plan it all out, so it didn't feel like we were driving any kind of agenda. It was just, 'Okay, here's all the elements we've got going — let's just make stories.'"

But, of course, the best-laid plans of mice and television producers are there for the higher powers to play with. Besides the general pressures of taking over as show runners, Mallozzi and Mullie found themselves dealing with several other considerable challenges. For various reasons, the production had found it necessary to write out the character of Dr Elizabeth Weir, played by Torri Higginson. The decision had actually been made at the conclusion of season three. The writers had always found Weir a difficult character to integrate into the Atlantis environment, with all its inherent jeopardy — as a civilian diplomat with no military background, Weir's function as part of the Pegasus Project was difficult to flesh out. Finding reasons to take her off-world and into the heart of a story could easily feel contrived. Yet having her be the character that stayed in the city watching the teams come and go did not make for a fulfilling role, either for the writers or for Higginson. Eventually, the producers felt the only solution was to replace the character. So, coming into season four, one of the first decisions that the writing team had to make was who should fill Weir's shoes.

"A lot of people think we decided to bring in Carter and then moved Weir out," says Martin Gero. "Actually, we decided to move Weir out and then had a long meeting about who should be that base commander."

Amanda Tapping's name wasn't the only one that formed part of this debate. The list included stars that had never previously been connected to the world of *Stargate*, as well as some that loomed large in the series' history.

Below: Will the real Carson Beckett (Paul McGillion) please stand up...

"Beau Bridges," says Gero, naming one. "Richard Dean Anderson was probably mentioned at some point, though never realistically! But we just got really excited about the idea of Carter. I never doubted for a second that it was going to be great. She's the perfect person to run Atlantis: she's got the science background, she's got the military background, she's incredibly well respected by all the characters on our side of the franchise. It just made all the sense in the world."

"I know a lot of the fans originally were somewhat reticent when they heard that Amanda was coming over," acknowledges Paul Mullie. "She was such a strong presence on *SG-1*, I think that they feared she would overshadow our established characters in *Atlantis*. But from the get-go, we'd always planned for her to be more of a Hammond or a Landry character. Carter would come in and be in command of the expedition, but she would be the one that would stay back, the one the team would report to. On the other hand, if we wanted to go off-world we had reason to involve her,

because she had the military background. It was unbelievably easy to let her become part of that world. It really just happened on its own, we didn't have to force it. It would have been far harder to write a new character. The only reason I was even comfortable with the idea of Torri not being there was because I knew that Amanda could slip into that role really, really easily. She's already established, the audience already knew her, we didn't have to make a new character, and her character fit in so many ways."

"Her addition to the show was just a godsend," says writer/producer Carl Binder, who found himself writing for Carter properly for the first time. "I just loved what Amanda brought to the show, as a person and as an actress. That character was a joy to write for. I didn't get to write a lot for her in 'Lifeline' or 'Missing', but I got to really

Above: Season four allowed the producers to bring in some familiar faces.

Above: Jeannie Miller (Kate Hewlett) lends her brother a hand... again.

have fun with her in 'Quarantine'. What she brings to every scene she's in is just so perfectly performed and effortless. I can't say enough about how happy I was to have her on the show."

What wasn't quite so easy about the decision to integrate Carter into *Stargate: Atlantis* was what it meant for John Lenic and N. John Smith, charged with organising the shooting schedules. Although for the first time *Stargate: Atlantis* and *Stargate SG-1* were not both shooting a full series, the *Stargate SG-1* movies, *Ark of Truth* and *Continuum*, were scheduled to be in production. To complicate matters further, the two movies were on very inflexible schedules of their own, and would also tie up the visual effects department on both shows as production continued. And with Amanda Tapping now starring in both the movies and *Stargate: Atlantis*, things became quite challenging. On top of all that, three members of the *Atlantis* cast were expecting new additions to their families. David Hewlett and Jason Momoa were both due to become fathers during filming, and would obviously need time off-set around those happy events. Most complicated, however, was star actress Rachel Luttrell's pregnancy.

"That was a shock at the top of the year," recalls Lenic. "We weren't expecting it. It was fantastic, and I love Rachel, but her pregnancy was more and more difficult to shoot around, because she kept growing! You had to shoot everything with her inside the episodic schedule, because if you held anything with her for even a couple of weeks, you would see a difference. So it was really difficult."

The producers had already realised that because of the movies' schedules, quite a few episodes of season four were going to have to be shot out of order. And Luttrell would now only be available for part of the year.

"It was really just about getting out a calendar and going, 'Okay, when are you due? So you can work up to here...'" laughs Mullie. "We had realised that we were going to have to do a lot of shooting out of order, which became increasingly problematic because she had a definite continuity which we didn't necessarily follow!"

A decision that helped the production a lot was to make Luttrell's pregnancy part of the season's arc. Teyla would also carry a child, allowing much more scope in the year's production. Incorporating Teyla's pregnancy meant that the costume department would only have to hide Luttrell's growing stomach in the episodes shot

Below: Actress Rachel Luttrell's pregnancy produced some interesting creative opportunities for the writers.

out of sequence, and the show's directors wouldn't have to think up imaginative ways of hiding her belly on screen. It also gave the writers a whole new slew of stories to play with.

"We had already had an idea to do a Teyla arc, because we felt that her character was drifting to the sidelines a little bit," explains Paul Mullie. "So we were going to have the Athosians missing. Then Rachel came in on the first week of production and said, 'I'm pregnant.' So that got layered into the story and became a nice arc — and not just for her character, because it became the overall arc for the season. We tied it in with Michael, and he became the recurring villain. We already knew we wanted to do an arc for her, but we didn't know exactly what it was going to be. Michael was going to take the Athosians, and that was all we really knew, so the pregnancy got layered into that."

"The season has a great arc from beginning to end for a bunch of reasons," says Martin Gero, "some by design, some not by design. It was a rare thing that we knew exactly where we were going the whole year, and Rachel's pregnancy forced our hand that way. We knew we were going to do something with her people, but with Rachel actually getting pregnant it added a level of complication that we needed. It gave the whole season a connective fibre that we rarely have."

Though the creative aspects of the pregnancy had opened many doors for the writers, a film set isn't the best place for an expectant mother — particularly one who's usually in the thick of the on-screen action.

"Before she got pregnant, she was doing her own stunts. Rachel couldn't do that anymore, so we needed to be sensitive to that and bring in a stunt double," says John Lenic, whose job partly involves finding such stand-ins. "We had her stunt double wear a pregnancy pad so it also looked like she was pregnant, which worked out very well. Her stamina, as well, we had to watch for. When you're not pregnant, you can go for twelve hours a day. Of course you're tired, but you can still do it. When you're pregnant it takes so much more out of you. You're *so* tired. But she really pulled through, and it was great. The hardest thing was the continuity in the size of her belly."

The season also introduced another new character in the shape of Jewel Staite's Dr Jennifer Keller. Her's was a face that had been seen briefly at the conclusion of season three, but in season four the character would really come into her own.

"She was in 'Instinct', which was crazy because we took Jewel Staite and completely covered her face with horrible monster make-up!" says Paul Mullie, recalling the season two episode where Staite played Ellia, a young Wraith. "I did a rewrite of that, and I just remember thinking, 'I can't believe I'm covering Jewel Staite's face with this ridiculous make-up — we've got to bring her back as a human.' So she'd always been someone that we'd had in mind for various parts. It was just a 'right place, right time' kind of thing. We needed a doctor, and she was the right

Above: Jewel Staite joined the cast as Dr Jennifer Keller.

choice for us. She happened to be available and wanted to do it. She's a fantastic actress, and a nice addition to the dynamic. We didn't really know exactly how we wanted her character to be right away — you never do when you're writing a new character, so you just have to feel it out. Carl wrote 'Missing' early on and Keller had a big role in it. When we watched the dailies for that, we saw Keller in that and it was just, 'Oh my god, this is going to work. She's just awesome.'"

Despite the challenges that producing season four brought, the team behind *Stargate: Atlantis* managed to pull off a brilliant season of television, one of the show's best yet.

"I'm very proud of season four," states writer/producer Carl Binder. "I really like the way it turned out. It's really nice to see how the season-long arc played out and came together."

For Mallozzi and Mullie, though, the year is a bit of a blur. "It was a really crazy year for us," says Mullie. "I don't think we were quite prepared for it. We had done producing before, but up to that point it was much more creative — about the writing and then getting into the meetings and getting it on screen. It's all the stuff that we have to deal with [as show runners] that has nothing to do with what goes on the screen that really wears you down after a while. It saps the creative side quite a bit — it takes so much energy just doing the day-to-day stuff that it colours the whole season for me," he laughs. "I just remember being tired the whole time!" Å

THE EPISODES

"This is either the most elaborate practical joke of all time, or I'm in serious trouble here." — *Sheppard*

SEASON 4 REGULAR CAST:

Joe Flanigan (Colonel John Sheppard)

Amanda Tapping (Colonel Samantha Carter)

David Hewlett (Dr Rodney McKay)

Rachel Luttrell (Teyla Emmagan)

Jason Momoa (Ronon Dex)

ADRIFT

WRITTEN BY: Martin Gero
DIRECTED BY: Martin Wood

GUEST CAST: Torri Higginson (Dr Elizabeth Weir), David Nykl (Dr Radek Zelenka), Chuck Campbell (Technician), Jewel Staite (Dr Jennifer Keller), Linda Ko (Marie), Bill Dow (Dr Bill Lee), Michael Beach (Colonel Abe Ellis), Gerry Durand (Captain Levine)

As Dr Weir is rushed to sickbay, McKay and Zelenka realize the city is losing power, and they need to find a way to stop the strain on the ZPM. The extremities of Atlantis begin to decompress as the city consolidates its energy. McKay can't stop it, and some people are unable to make it to safety. McKay recommends abandoning all shields except those protecting the tower, and Sheppard agrees. Meanwhile, Colonel Ellis contacts Colonel Carter aboard the Midway Station, and she realizes something has gone drastically wrong in the Pegasus Galaxy. Dr Keller attempts brain surgery to ease Weir's cranial swelling. McKay realizes that the hyperdrive is still working, and sends Zelenka to fix the power conduits. He doesn't have time before Atlantis enters an asteroid belt, and despite Sheppard's efforts the hyperdrive is damaged, forcing Zelenka and Sheppard to go outside the shield to fix it. McKay comes up with a plan to save Weir by using the nanites to recreate the damaged sections of her brain and, in Sheppard's absence, tells Keller to go ahead. Zelenka manages to repair the hyperdrive but it's too late — the city has already lost too much power to activate it. Sheppard returns to discover a half-Replicator Weir, as horrified at her new existence as he is. Carter, realizing that there is a way to track Atlantis through the gate, heads for the Pegasus Galaxy. In Atlantis, they decide to use the last remaining power to stage a heist — namely, stealing a ZPM from the Asuran homeworld…

McKAY: You're a genius.
KELLER: Well, you know, trying to save a life and whatnot.

Replacing a much-loved and long-standing character is no easy feat. Faced with the necessity of writing out Elizabeth Weir, the producers had thought long and hard about how to bring in the next leader of Atlantis. It had to feel organic, and the audience's intimacy with the incoming character could not be forced. To some extent, choosing to incorporate Sam Carter of *SG-1* had given the writers a head start on that score — she was an established character, one that they didn't have to find a voice for from scratch. But there was still the issue of how to introduce her to Atlantis without her arrival seeming too sudden or contrived. To do that, it was decided that though Carter would be seen in the season opener, she wouldn't set foot in the city itself.

Opposite: Sheppard prepares to save Atlantis yet again.

"We wanted to just keep her alive in 'Adrift'," explains writer Martin Gero, "and remind the audience that she's there. Thankfully, we found a super-cool location like the Midway Space Station. It made all the sense in the world that she be the one that finds Atlantis. In the end, I think the transition was fairly seamless. There were some Torri supporters that were disappointed, but Carter's a great character and had the most history in Atlantis. She's been around since season one. She was in 'Letters from Pegasus', she was in 'Grace Under Pressure', she was in 'McKay and Mrs Miller'. So she had a presence in that canon of story-telling."

The writers also had to find a way to establish another new character whom the audience would be seeing a lot of — Dr Jennifer Keller. Though she'd been seen at the conclusion of season three, it had been only briefly. Now she needed to really make her presence felt.

"I really liked the duality of trying to save Weir and save the city," says Gero. "Those are the storylines that raced through the entire episode. That's one of the things that I'm proudest of, the inter-cutting between McKay trying to bring the city to life and Keller trying to bring Weir back to life. That's also the first meat that we've given Keller, in 'Adrift'."

KELLER: McKay! I've been trying to reach you.
McKAY: Well I've been trying to save the city and whatnot.

For director Martin Wood, having Keller, the incoming character, be the physician trying to heal Weir, the outgoing character, had a symmetry that really worked.

"What I wanted to do was make sure that the audience — and Torri — didn't feel like they were short-shrifted. It was difficult, because Torri came in knowing that she wasn't going to be a regular, and that was a bittersweet thing for her. I know that as much trouble as Torri was having with where she was going with the character and feeling that she wasn't stretching very far, having to leave something that you've been involved with for so long is still bittersweet. And the audience was going to feel the same way. So for me, it was very fitting that the new character was the one that was working on the old character, trying to save her."

The scenes in which Keller operates on the dying Weir were particularly complicated. Wood wanted to make the brain surgery look as realistic as possible. Of course, they couldn't ask actress Torri Higginson to shave her head for real. Instead, the production managed to find a woman with matching hair color who was willing to shave her head to raise money for a cancer charity. Having achieved those shots, Wood moved on to the operation itself.

"I had to show a brain operation without really showing a brain operation," the director explains. "We actually had a brain surgeon there, and we had a prosthetic brain. The camera that you see in behind Weir — that camera's actually pointed at the

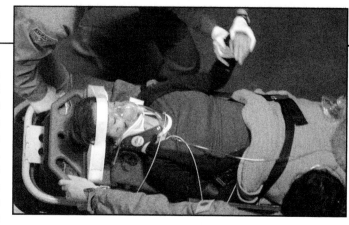

prosthetic brain, with the real brain surgeon's hands doing the real operation. He's actually doing what he would normally be doing for this brain op. So I put a camera on him and that's what's feeding the monitor that you see. That whole scene, he was talking to Jewel so that she could copy what he was doing, and you saw it translate from the brain monitor to her hands. Torri was there with a full head of hair, lying there and being operated on for an hour!"

Besides the emotional issues surrounding Weir's sickness and Higginson's imminent departure, 'Adrift' also managed to pack in an astounding amount of action-adventure material. For the first time, the audience got to see inside the almost-completed Midway Station, for example.

"I had a very specific way that I wanted to look at Midway," says Wood. "It was a very expensive shot but I thought it was important to show both gates to remind us where we were. I wanted to make it bigger than it was, and unfortunately the budget wouldn't allow it. But I love the fact that when we get into it, it has less gravity."

Of course, for the actors in that scene, Amanda Tapping and Bill Dow, the lack of gravity meant being fitted with a harness and spun in the air. It's something Tapping had done many times during her days on *Stargate SG-1*, but for Dow, who had only limited experience in such a rig, it was something of a challenge.

"This one was tricky because they could only have one pick-up point," explains Dow, who with 'Adrift' saw his character, Dr Lee, transfer to *Stargate: Atlantis*. "When you see those *Peter Pan*-type things, they've got at least two and sometimes more pick-up points, so that the weight is more evenly distributed and you've got a little bit of control of it. But with this one it was more like I was just being picked up by the scruff of the neck," he says, laughing.

"That episode was an enormous amount of fun to do because so much happened," says Martin Gero. "Every act there's a big event. One of the things that I wanted to try to do in general — and sometimes it worked and sometimes it didn't — was to start doing teasers for the next episode in the previous episode. 'Adrift' is one of those early episodes where we had time to figure that out. Act five could very easily be act one of the next episode. It's also just a super-tense episode from beginning to end. Our characters are under an enormous strain. One of my favorite scenes is the confrontation between Sheppard and McKay when McKay decides to reactivate Weir's nanites. That's stuff that we don't get to do a lot of, except in those heightened situations. Plus it had my favorite visual effects shot of the whole season, that space walk shot that goes 360 degrees — that really turned out great." Å

Above: Not everyone survived the events of 'Adrift' unscathed.

LIFELINE

WRITTEN BY: Carl Binder
DIRECTED BY: Martin Wood

GUEST CAST: Torri Higginson (Dr Elizabeth Weir), David Nykl (Dr Radek Zelenka), Michael Beach (Colonel Abe Ellis), Bill Dow (Dr Bill Lee), David Ogden Stiers (Oberoth)

McKay and Zelenka work on getting Atlantis's drive functioning well enough for their planned raid. McKay suggests that Weir could help — her nanites could hack into the Asuran systems. Sheppard wants a failsafe, and McKay assures him that the nanites can be turned off, though that will kill Elizabeth. Weir agrees to the mission instantly. As the heist gets under way in the Pegasus Galaxy, in Earth's galaxy Carter and Dr Lee meet with the *Apollo* to search for Atlantis. Weir guides Ronon and Sheppard successfully to the ZPM. They're on their way back when McKay discovers a disabled order that will pit the Replicators against the Wraith if he can reactivate it. Trick is he'd have to wait until the Asurans next share their programming, and there's no knowing when that will be. Sheppard tells him no, so McKay finds a way of storing the command instead, but that involves directly accessing the Replicator computer core. McKay turns the puddle-jumper's shield into an anti-Replicator field and Sheppard and Ronon head out again, leaving McKay to keep an eye on Weir in case he needs to disable her nanites. Oberoth detects the jumper but they can't penetrate the shield. Sheppard and Ronon, having reached the core, can't get McKay's data tablet to work properly. He begins to talk them through it, but the Replicators have managed to bypass the field. Weir senses this, and leaves. McKay tries to activate her kill switch, but nothing happens. Sheppard manages to complete the programming as the Replicators enter, but they freeze before they can open fire. It's Weir, who has connected with the Replicator collective and has distracted Oberoth. Sheppard and McKay find her, but she warns that she can't hold them for long and tells them to leave without her. McKay, Ronon and Sheppard take off in the jumper but are intercepted by an Asuran cruiser. They're only saved when the *Apollo* arrives. Back in the city, they find a planet Weir had no knowledge of, and settle Atlantis onto its ocean.

Opposite: Elizabeth Weir (Torri Higginson) meets her nemesis (David Ogden Stiers) — and prepares to make the ultimate sacrifice.

SHEPPARD: How much time do we have?
McKAY: Let's not start that again.

Viewers don't often get to see the characters of *Stargate: Atlantis* engaging in nefarious deeds, least of all a heist designed to 'liberate' an item from the possession of an enemy. Which is exactly why writer/producer Carl Binder thought it was a great idea for an episode.

"We were all sitting around pitching ideas about what we wanted to do," he explains of the pre-season planning stages. "One of the ideas that I wanted to do was 'Missing', and the other was a heist. I said, 'I would love to do a heist where the mission is we have to go into this place that's impossible, steal this thing and get out, and something goes wrong.' Everybody liked that idea, but what could it be?"

As the writers talked further and broke the story, the idea of the team having to steal a ZPM came into play. And with that, the beginning of the season began to take on a much more solid shape.

"All of a sudden we realized that this could be paired up with 'Adrift', which wasn't called 'Adrift' at the time. We could go into the Replicator homeworld, and we could spread out the resolution of us being stranded in space because we need to find a ZPM in order to land the city. So it was integrated into that, and the first episode became this A-parter. Then we spread out Carter coming to Atlantis over two episodes rather than wrapping it up in one episode. It let us have a little more fun with it."

SHEPPARD: How's it going boys?
McKAY: Well, we'd be making a lot more progress if Timmy Torture wasn't trying to kill me every two seconds.

Another major aspect of 'Lifeline' became how to write out one of the show's regular cast members, as during the events of 'Lifeline', viewers would be asked to let go of one of *Stargate: Atlantis*'s most important figures — Dr Elizabeth Weir. As civilian commander of the city, Weir had made many personal sacrifices to lead the Atlantis crew. This episode would see her final, and most significant, sacrifice.

"I specifically wanted to write that episode," explains Carl Binder, who penned the third part of a story that had begun with season three's 'First Strike' and continued in 'Adrift'. Binder has often said how much he enjoyed the character of Weir, and so writing her send-off carried particular significance for him. "I wanted to write the episode in which we said goodbye to her and that all worked into this episode. That was a bonus for me. I really wanted to make sure, when we were breaking the story, that she went out in a heroic way — that she gave herself in order to let us escape. So it was nice to give her that kind of send-off."

In actual fact, it was Weir's physical state that allowed the writing team to accomplish the heist plot. "We were going to go into the Replicator city and steal a ZPM. How is this possible? And we said, 'Well, we have Weir, she has the nanites, she can connect with the city.' So that's how it all worked into the plot, because we knew we had to write Torri out, we just weren't quite sure how we were going to do that. That just all fell into place and allowed for a really nice send-off for the character. It also kept it kind of nebulous as to whether she really has gone or whether we could bring

her back. That's the great thing about science fiction, you never really quite know."

Though she would later return to the character, for actress Torri Higginson what was happening to Weir in 'Lifeline' was far more clear-cut. As far as Higginson is concerned, as soon as Weir discovered just how it was that she came to be whole again, she accepted death.

"She absolutely fast-forwarded to the inevitable," the actress states. "She knew how difficult it was to get rid of the nanites, and she knew how hard it would be to be a part of her world with that threat inside her. So she was just looking for a way to help as much as she could before she had to separate herself from everyone. I think that was the weight on her for that whole episode — there were scenes where she was just sitting there quietly, thinking about that." Å

Above: Three heads are better than one... especially when they're these heads.

REUNION

WRITTEN BY: Joseph Mallozzi & Paul Mullie
DIRECTED BY: William Waring

GUEST CAST: David Nykl (Dr Radek Zelenka), Scott Heindl (Male Wraith), Mark Dacascos (Tyre), Byron Lucas (Replicator), Christopher Judge (Teal'c), Aleks Paunovic (Rakai), Kyra Zagorsky (Ara), Arran Landry (Townsperson), Rob Avery (Lieutenant Miller)

Ronon is overjoyed when he is reunited with Tyre, Rakai and Ara — old friends of his from the Satedan armed forces who survived the Wraith attack. On Atlantis, Sheppard and the team learn that Colonel Samantha Carter is to take Weir's place as the city's new commander. One of her first moves once she's arrived is to refuse Ronon's request to bring the Satedans back to Atlantis. They ask an angry Ronon to join them instead. He considers it, and in the meantime asks Sheppard to help him to create a distraction so his friends can raid a Wraith lab. The Wraith are trying to override the Replicator code that McKay activated. The joint mission does not go well. A Wraith patrol overpowers Sheppard and Teyla. Rodney hides, but comes out when the Satedans appear — and is promptly handed over to the Wraith. Ronon makes it back to Atlantis and Carter prepares to lead a strike team to rescue Sheppard, Teyla and Rodney, and finish the mission. The Wraith want McKay to reprogram the code he changed so that the Replicators will cease their attack, and they have one in custody to test on. Meanwhile, Carter's attack works and the team liberate Sheppard and Teyla, while Ronon goes his own way. Discovering his Satedan friends with a Wraith, he demands to know the truth. His worst fears are realized when they reveal that they are now Wraith worshippers. They beg him to join them, but Ronon refuses and a huge fight ensues, during which Rakai and Ara are killed. Tyre escapes, and Ronon finally realizes where his real home is: Atlantis.

CARTER: So I can expect you guys to come and visit sometime?
TEAL'C: Undomesticated equines could not keep me away.

It had been a while since Ronon's history had taken center stage, and for season four, the executive producers decided it was high time they returned to his Satedan roots. "I wanted to do it because we very rarely explore people's backstories," explains Joseph Mallozzi, who wrote the script. "And Ronon had such an interesting one — Rob [Cooper] did such a terrific job of exploring it in 'Sateda'. We had kind of established Ronon as the 'outlaw' Satedan on the run, and I thought it would be interesting if there were other Satedans out there who were just as kick-ass as him."

Opposite: John Sheppard realizes all is not well.

Of course, this being *Stargate: Atlantis*, things are never quite as simple as they seem! True to form, the writing staff came up with a way of making Ronon's longed-for reunion with his lost friends just a little more complicated.

"It was Carl [Binder] who pitched out the possibility that maybe they were Wraith worshippers, and how would that affect Ronon," the writer recalls. "I thought that was kind of interesting."

In actual fact, 'Reunion' provided a real catalyst in the development of Ronon's character. Since joining the team in season two, he's always found himself living on the edge of Atlantis, isolated by his own feeling of being an outsider. But here, the character is given the chance to be a part of his old circle of friends again — and discovers something valuable about his connection with Sheppard and the team.

"Ronon is such a loyal individual, and it took him a while to trust our team," says Mallozzi. "But eventually, when he does trust our team, he would give his life for Sheppard and company. And I thought, 'What if he's faced with a real dilemma? What if he is faced with a choice between the loyalties of the past and the loyalties of the present?'"

Being in this place of torn loyalties cast Ronon into a very dark place for a while, in a trend that perpetuated throughout much of the season. Time and again we see characters questioning themselves and their place in the Pegasus Galaxy. Mallozzi confirms that both he and writing partner (and fellow show runner) Paul Mullie see the value in those types of stories.

CARTER: Ronon, where are your friends?
RONON: They're right here. Let's go home.

"I've always preferred the darker stories," Mallozzi says. "Overall, I think season four *is* darker than previous seasons — it's something we set out to do. One of the throughlines that we never got to pursue, although it turned out well in the end, was the Teyla storyline. We actually wanted her to go to the dark side, and we had the idea of her people going missing and her being so consumed by trying to find them that she goes to a dark place that we know has always been there for her, but her people disappearing just precipitates a complete descent. We ended up seeing a little of that in 'Missing', when you see her display almost a ruthless warrior mentality. But there are dark moments elsewhere as well. In 'Miller's Crossing' we see a very, *very* dark Sheppard moment — the lengths the man will go to to save his friends. I know that was controversial: fans thought maybe he'd stepped over the line and I don't know, maybe he did. But I've always liked characters that have a bit of darkness about them, [but] that aren't necessarily outright bad guys."

'Reunion' also saw the arrival of Sam Carter, in a piece of symmetry that Mallozzi feels worked particularly well for the start of the season. "While I was pursuing the

Ronon story, what I wanted to do was establish Carter as the command presence," he explains. "I realized that thematically, their situations are not that dissimilar. On the one hand you have Ronon and his choice between the past, present and possibly his future on Atlantis, and on the other hand we have Carter, who's faced with a similar choice. The A and B stories came together quite nicely in this episode.

"In terms of guest stars, it was great to get Chris," Mallozzi continues. "I thought we needed to ground Carter at the SGC, to see her leave and come over. I wanted someone to personify ten years of SG-1, and I can think of no one better than Chris Judge. We just wanted him to come in for one scene, and I said, 'Really, we'd love you to do this, but it's just one scene and we're just looking to pay a cameo fee...' Even before I could get into it, he said, 'Forget it, whatever you guys need, I'll be here.' So he did that for us. And as a result of him being so kind and generous with his time I said, 'Guys we've got to come up with an episode where we team Ronon and Teal'c.' So we ended up doing 'Midway'."

Of 'Reunion', Mallozzi has only good things to say. "Across the board, it was a very good episode. Mark Dacascos came in and did a great job as Tyre, the troubled Satedan. Mark is a great guy, and I wanted him because he has a martial arts background, and I know he, Jason and BamBam had a great time putting together that fight. Unfortunately, as always happens, there's never enough time to rehearse and there's never enough time to shoot, so the fights get truncated. But I think it was one of the best fights we've done on the show. I think it was a very satisfying episode for Jason — he really enjoyed doing it." Å

Above: Ronon and Teyla Emmagan (Rachel Luttrell) toast the Satedan survivors.

DOPPELGANGER

WRITTEN BY: Robert C. Cooper

DIRECTED BY: Robert C. Cooper

GUEST CAST: David Nykl (Dr Radek Zelenka), Kavan Smith (Major Evan Lorne), Jewel Staite (Dr Jennifer Keller), Claire Rankin (Dr Kate Heightmeyer), Linda Ko (Marie), Yee Jee Tso (Technician)

Whilst on a routine mission, Sheppard is compelled to touch a strange crystal attached to a tree. On contact a blast knocks him to the ground, but he is unhurt. That night Teyla suffers from an horrific dream in which she sees Sheppard as a part-Wraith that feeds on her. Then Keller too has a vivid nightmare in which Sheppard brings Teyla into the infirmary. While Keller examines her, a creature bursts out of Teyla's stomach. Waking up, a disturbed Keller goes to get herself a sleep aid. Ronon and Sheppard arrive — they've been sparring and Ronon needs stitching up yet again. While Keller works on him he falls asleep, and has a violent nightmare in which Sheppard is trying to bury him alive. The next day Keller takes the story of these three dreams to Carter. Whilst in her office, a security alert sounds. A sleepwalking Major Lorne is holding Sheppard at gunpoint, accusing him of being a Replicator. Carter sends a team to retrieve another crystal. They discover that it holds an entity, and that Sheppard must have brought one back to Atlantis with the first crystal. Then Dr Heightmeyer dies — after having a nightmare in which Sheppard threw her over a balcony. Zelenka and Keller trace the entity as it moves, stopping finally at Sheppard. In his dream, Sheppard fights a losing battle with a perverted version of himself, until McKay finds a way to get into Sheppard's subconscious and tells him that the entity is vulnerable to electric shock. Keller shocks him, and his dream-doppelganger is distracted long enough for Sheppard to force him through the gate. In the real world, the entity returns to the crystal, and the team returns both crystals to the planet — leaving before they can be lured into touching any more.

McKAY: Last night, I dreamt that Colonel Carter invited me to her quarters for dinner.

TEYLA: Maybe you shouldn't be telling us this, Rodney.

KELLER: Yeah, I said nightmare, not delusional male fantasy.

"I guess I've always been fascinated with what scares people," says Robert Cooper, who both wrote and directed 'Doppelganger'. "It's a bit of a sci-fi chestnut to do the episode where everyone explores their fears, but it was something *I* had not done before, and I wanted to do an episode that would give me an opportunity, as a director, to have some fun and play around with filmmaking techniques."

Opposite: Sheppard finds himself in an unfamiliar situation.

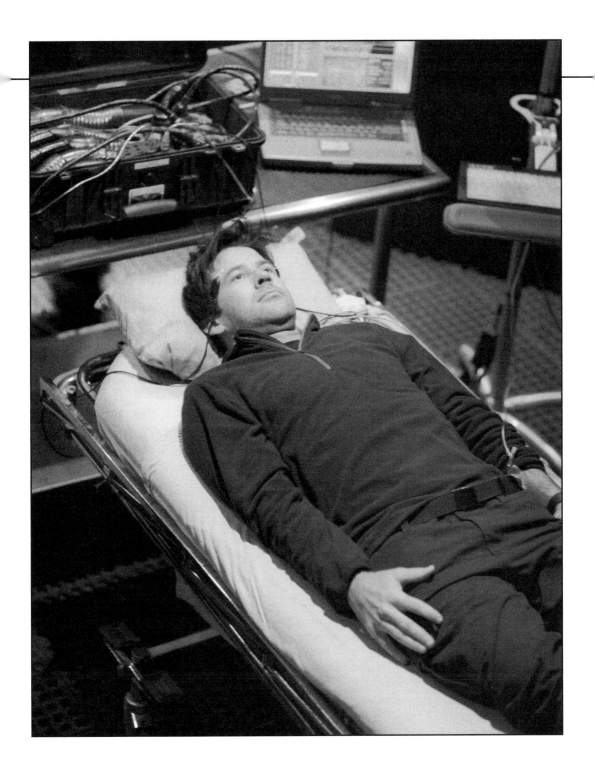

In the event, 'Doppelganger' turned into one of the creepiest episodes of *Stargate: Atlantis* to date. It made use of an alien entity that some viewers would be familiar with from the *Stargate SG-1* season one episode 'Cold Lazarus'.

"It's always a challenge when you're spinning a story," says Cooper. "Okay, I have something that I think is worth bringing to the table — seeing Sheppard as the bad guy, manipulating people's dreams and revealing what their various fears are. That's fun, that's worth doing, but what's the science fiction mechanism for that? Sometimes you get accused of recycling old ideas or stories. Or you could say, I'm looking at things that exist within the franchise. This is a world that exists. That's something that I think has really drawn people to *Stargate*, because the world integrates and it feels like something that pops up here may play out there. It was also a way of getting into the story quicker. Instead of spending a lot of time developing a new concept of the entity that's causing the problem, you use some element that's been pre-established and then get on with the fun of the story."

One of the most disturbing aspects of the episode is seeing Colonel Sheppard as a menacing influence. The audience is used to seeing him play the hero, not the antagonist, and combined with Cooper's method of shooting, the effect is particularly discomforting. For star Joe Flanigan, playing both versions of himself was a challenge.

McKAY: Wait and listen. Turns out she was serving lemon chicken. I mean, *lemon*. And the only reason she invited me to dinner was to tell me she was promoting Zelenka over me.
RONON: That's it?
McKAY: Then I was eaten by a whale.

"It was very important to him to find a way to make them distinct and separate them in his mind," says Cooper. "I think that's always a tough thing for an actor. When they play a different role in a different show or movie, that's another context. But when you're on screen literally opposite the character you're normally playing, there's a direct comparison between the two. That's a real mind freak! I can't act in any way, so I certainly sympathize," adds the director. "It's tough. There's no question that there is a unique talent required to pull it off."

When it came to directing the script that he had written, Cooper discovered that he had made something of a rod for his own back. He'd thought that writing an episode featuring dream sequences would allow him to create some unique effects, but that didn't quite work out the way he'd planned.

"It's funny because I thought, 'Oh, I'll do an episode that has nightmares in them and I'll be able to play around with the way in which we shoot those.' But the twist of

the script is that you're not quite sure if these things are really happening. So if I went that far outside the box as a director, you would know immediately that it was a dream. I kind of hooked myself," he laughs. "My original intention was to have all this freedom to do all this cool stuff, and then as a writer I kind of screwed me! That was the challenge as a director, to decide how to shoot this so that it felt a little bit dreamy and surreal but at the same time told the story."

The episode also needed a real shock — beyond the general creepiness of seeing Sheppard — to add a measure of gravitas that would extend beyond the episode's conclusion. The solution came in the death of Claire Heightmeyer, the expedition's resident psychologist.

"To me, the number one problem of writing an action-adventure series from week to week is finding a way to create jeopardy for your characters, who you know for the most part are going to survive at the end of the episode," Cooper explains. "Having a bad dream is not all that scary. There's got to be a way to bring that jeopardy into the real world, and when you were a kid, everyone always said if you die in your dream, you die for real. So I wanted to include that. And if we had just killed a 'red shirt' then the reaction of the characters wouldn't have had as much impact, because suddenly everyone gets all upset about some guy we've never met before dying, and it feels phony, it doesn't feel right. It was also one of the earlier episodes for Carter, and I thought that would create a good opportunity to show her leadership skills."

Coming early in the season, 'Doppelganger' set the tone for the year, which took a somewhat darker turn. Right from the opening scenes, the atmosphere is moody and claustrophobic, a look that Cooper was very pleased with and which contributed to his overall satisfaction with the episode.

"The look was something that [director of photography] Jim Menard worked on very hard, and he did a great job. It's got an appropriate creepiness factor when necessary, and I think that everyone's performances are very strong." Å

TRAVELERS

WRITTEN BY: Joseph Mallozzi & Paul Mullie
DIRECTED BY: William Waring

GUEST CAST: Kavan Smith (Major Evan Lorne), Scott Heindl (Male Wraith), Jill Wagner (Larrin), Chris Kalhoon (Crewman), Michael Cram (Silas), Sean Rogerson (Nevik)

En route to Atlantis following a solo mission, Sheppard's jumper is attacked by an unknown ship. He only just manages to tell Atlantis what's happening before he's taken aboard and the ship vanishes into hyperspace. Sheppard learns that his captors are nomads living only on their ships to avoid the Wraith. Their leader, Larrin, wants to retro-engineer an interface from Sheppard's Ancient genes. Showing him an Ancient battlecruiser, she demands that he make it work for them. But Sheppard takes the ship into hyperspace and broadcasts a signal, hoping to tell Atlantis where he is. Larrin forces Sheppard to surrender, but Sheppard's signal has attracted a Wraith hive. Larrin has no choice but to let him take control again, and Sheppard uses the drones to destroy the hive, but not before they've blasted the ship and killed Larrin's people. Sheppard locks her up and contacts Atlantis, who send a team to retrieve him. Larrin escapes, but Wraith board the battlecruiser and Sheppard and the woman have to work together. They defeat the Wraith, and Larrin thanks Sheppard with a kiss — but she stuns him, still intending to keep him for his genes. More of her fleet arrive, and so does McKay's team. They prepare to attack to stop the ships entering hyperspace, but Sheppard brokers an alliance between Larrin's people and Atlantis against the Wraith. She finally agrees, and lets him go… though Sheppard is sure they'll meet again.

SHEPPARD: Sure you want to go through with this? If you don't make it, I'm going to feel responsible, and, well, I really don't need the guilt.
LARRIN: We'll be fine as long as you don't shoot too early. I'm sure that's not the first time you've heard that from a woman.

'Travelers' was the brainchild of show runner and executive producer Paul Mullie. The episode explored more about just how human life has managed to survive in the Pegasus Galaxy despite the ever-present threat of culling by the Wraith. It also gave star Joe Flanigan a solo outing as Sheppard struggles against two foes — the feisty Larrin and old enemies the Wraith — without his team.

"With 'Travelers', two things stand out for me," says Mullie. "First, the basic concept. One of the problems with the set-up of the series is that, since the Wraith

Opposite: The Wraith encounter more resistance than they bargained for.

don't allow any of the human populations in the galaxy to get too advanced, we very rarely encounter anybody with technology that can match our own. So I conceived of the idea of people who hid from the Wraith by staying in space all the time. I also liked the idea that these people were existing on very old tech that had been repaired a thousand times over and was now beginning to fail them. This gave us a reason to get Atlantis — or more precisely Sheppard — into the story."

It's often said that where an episode is set is an additional character in the story, and that's certainly the case in 'Travelers'. As Mullie noted, most cultures visited by the Atlantis team are necessarily less technologically advanced than the team from Earth, and are also generally planet-based. By making Larrin's people a space-dwelling society, Mullie created the opportunity to see something a bit different. Besides giving Sheppard a cohort as technologically savvy as himself, which allows for a different relationship than we've seen the colonel have before, it also gave the art department the chance to have some fun.

SHEPPARD: Nice ship. Little bit of a fixer-upper, but I can see the potential. I'm not talking about anything drastic. Maybe just a paint job, some throw pillows...

"It was an excuse to build a cool set," the writer admits, "which is the second thing that stands out in my mind from that episode. The Travelers' ship set was one of my all-time favorites. It was really just a corridor with a small room on one end [the cell] and bigger room on the other [the room where Sheppard meets and talks to Larrin]. In fact, if I'm not mistaken, it was actually a modification of the set originally built for the season three episode 'The Ark'."

Although the set configuration itself was very simple, the ship really came alive once James Robbins' painters and set decorators got to work with creating the interior. No polished Ancient technology this — the Travelers' ship had to look as if it was tacked together from whatever the nomadic people could find on their endless journey through space.

"I just loved what our construction, paint and set decoration people did with it," says Mullie. "You really had to walk around in it and take a close look to see the attention to detail that was put into it. There were all these crazy alien tech units stuck on the walls that were actually made up of deconstructed and re-assembled toys and other pieces of miscellaneous gack. And then they added about ten miles of hoses and wires to really make it look like a ship that was barely able to fly."

"As well as the set decorating, the hoses, wires and consoles," adds *Stargate: Atlantis* construction coordinator Scott Wellenbrink, "it was extraordinarily good paint in the 'Travelers' set. It's like anything good — you build layers on top. James Robbins is good at layers!"

Above: He's really just too trusting, isn't he?

In fact, although he was happy with the finished episode, the appearance of this set remains Mullie's one bone of contention with 'Travelers'. As with so much of episodic television, there was no real time to appreciate the setting, and as a result, much of the hard work that went into the ship's interiors was lost.

"Unfortunately, the story wound up playing out in such a way that the set pretty much disappears from the action after the first act," says Mullie regretfully. "We all felt this was a shame, not least because of the money we'd spent on it — you don't want to know how much! So we vowed to bring it back. Of course, Larrin came back in 'Be All My Sins Remember'd', but still flying the Ancient ship, which made more sense. But we did finally find an excuse to revisit an updated and extended version of the set. We get to see the engine room and the bridge in a season five episode called 'The Lost Tribe'." Å

TABULA RASA

WRITTEN BY: Alan
McCullough
DIRECTED BY: Martin Wood

GUEST CAST: David Nykl (Dr Radek Zelenka), Brenda James (Dr
Katie Brown), Kavan Smith (Major Evan Lorne), Linda Ko
(Marie), Jewel Staite (Dr Jennifer Keller), Graem Beddoes
(Scientist), Joel Cottingham (Doctor), Zach Selwyn (Scientist
#2), Niall Matter (Lieutenant Kemp), D. Harlan Cutshall
(Marine), Robert Clark (Dr Gerald Baxter)

Chaos strikes Atlantis when a plant bacteria causes the city's personnel to lose their memories. The bacteria has spread throughout the city, and Sam — knowing that she is infected herself — orders Zelenka to remove the gate crystals, worried that someone in the throes of the illness may carry it elsewhere. Teyla and Ronon appear to be immune, and Teyla knows of a simple plant cure common in the Pegasus Galaxy. Unfortunately, Carter can't remember where the gate crystals are hidden. There are so many patients that Keller begins to use the mess hall, ordering Lorne and his staff to bring all new cases there. Rodney frantically works on a cure, knowing that sooner or later he will succumb too. Unable to use the gate, Ronon and Sheppard head for the mainland instead, but as they search, Sheppard also becomes confused and Ronon is forced to restrain him. As their memories unravel, the principle crew all forget their roles, their expertise and where they are in the universe. Only Teyla has the answers — and as McKay lets go of his last memories, he launches a last ditch attempt to keep one thread constant. Left with only a message telling him to find Teyla, McKay wanders the now menacing corridors of Atlantis — chased by a group of soldiers defending the city in the only way they know how.

TEYLA: You are a scientist, Rodney. That is what you care about, that is what you will hang on to the longest.
McKAY: Right. Right, so... wait a minute. Doesn't that make me a really bad person?

Right from the start, the premise of 'Tabula Rasa' is chilling. The idea of suddenly having everything you recognize removed from your memory, including your sense of self and your affinity with those around you, is truly terrifying. One of the most fascinating aspects of the episode is the way all the characters that we know so well react. Their minds are blank slates, wiped completely clean of all their usual behavior.

"One of the objectives of that episode was to reset so that our leads, our main characters, wouldn't necessarily be the ones driving the action at first," explains writer Alan McCullough. "There's that opening scene in the mess hall where you have a bunch of people we've never seen before stepping up and taking the lead, and our

Opposite: Rodney McKay
puzzles over the mystery
— without the use of his
brain.

leads are kind of hidden in the background. Then gradually, despite having lost their memories, their personalities, their natural inclinations, start to come out."

"I thought it was such a neat way to see the characters *out* of character," says David Hewlett. "As an actor you've got so much history with all these different characters, and when you have scenes with them [in that episode], all of a sudden you can't use any of that. So it was a really interesting dynamic. A perfect example would be the Zelenka stuff. Zelenka and McKay have a very specific dysfunctional relationship. McKay doesn't respect him and he feels downtrodden and hurt. Going into 'Tabula Rasa', all of a sudden, I'm scared of Zelenka. Which is very difficult to do. In fact, I think the hardest acting *ever…*"

The episode has a very sinister feel to it, partly achieved by playing on the audience's existing empathy with the characters. Something that comes as a particular shock is the idea of Major Lorne as the enemy. The normally easy-going, reliable soldier becomes a figure of fear in one of the most striking threads of the episode. "We wanted to create that menacing tone. Right from the start, that was how we broke the story, and we thought it would be neat to see Lorne as the bad character. And at first we don't know why. Later we realize that he's not really become evil, he's just trying to protect the base in the way that he thinks it should be protected."

It's Martin Wood's choices as a director, however, that really plunge the audience into the gothic atmosphere of the story. Shooting Atlantis, which viewers have seen from every possible angle over the past four years, in such a way as to seem a completely unknown and alien environment, is a considerable feat.

CARTER: All right. We'll just have to search room by room. I mean, how big could this place possibly be?

"What wasn't planned, and what made the episode fantastic is that when we were in the production meeting, Martin Wood came up with the idea of actually creating a different look. The present was all in that overly contrasted, washed-out look, with the lights bleeding and so on, and the past would be shot the way we normally shoot an episode. And little by little the two would blend together. I think that creating those two looks not only helped the episode clarity-wise — you could easily tell what time you were watching — but also creates such an eerie look."

"When [director of photography] Jim Menard and I were talking about it we said, 'Let's make it look like the sort of glassy-eye you get when you're feverish,'" the director explains of the look he used to achieve part of this effect. "It was actually an effect we shot on camera instead of doing it as a visual effect afterwards. It sort of puts a halo around lights, and it's that feeling of heat and fever and sweat, of being infected."

To turn Atlantis from a safe, comfortable and familiar place into a menacing maze of unknown corridors required something further. In fact, Wood altered the methods

he would usually use to shoot scenes inside the city, which instantly skewed the audience's perception of what they were seeing.

"Part of it became the angles that I shot it at," he says. "Where McKay comes walking out of his lab, for example, it's a very low, long, raking angle. You don't do that kind of angle normally — it's not a very flattering angle — but it shows off way more floor than there is anything else in the shot, and that tends to be what does it."

The episode remains a cast and crew favorite from season four, and writer Alan McCullough will retain fond memories of it despite its difficult creation.

"The most challenging thing was tracking," he confesses, "because it was written in two different time-lines, and you had the present day story that played out and then we were flashing back. And boy, it was difficult to track in your mind what was happening where! I remember, just before turning the script in I had a last-minute crisis of confidence. I took all the scenes, rearranged the script chronologically and read it to make sure that I hadn't made any mistakes. And sure enough I had," McCullough says, laughing. "I discovered some instances where people we had dealt with and had locked up in the past were now reappearing. I think in one case I had Teyla referring to Lorne's team as 'the soldiers' even though she hadn't lost her memory. It was a very challenging script to write. But it's one of my favorites from that year." Å

MISSING

WRITTEN BY: Carl Binder DIRECTED BY: Andy Mikita	GUEST CAST: Jewel Staite (Dr Jennifer Keller), Johann Helf (Nabel Golan), Danny Trejo (Omal)

Teyla takes Dr Keller to visit her people, and is herself eager to see Kanaan, an Athosian with whom she has been having a relationship. They arrive to find the settlement deserted and discover signs of an attack, and the planet has been invaded by a savage group of Bola Kai warriors. Fleeing, Keller injures her ankle, and though she and Teyla make it to the Stargate, the Bola Kai prevent them from dialing. The two women make a run for it into the woods, and Teyla warns Keller that the warriors will stop at nothing to find them. They head for a hunting blind to hide for the night, but Teyla is forced to fight when the Bola Kai catch up with them. Defeating their attackers, the two women discover a bound and injured prisoner. Keller treats him, and they discover that he is a Genii spy named Golan who saw the Wraith cull the Athosians. The group is attacked again and this time taken prisoner, but Golan escapes. Teyla urges Keller to be strong, as the Bola Kai will want information about Atlantis. Keller buys some time by giving the Bola Kai a fake gate address for the city. Meanwhile, Sheppard begins to worry about their late return, and takes a team to the planet. Golan attacks and frees the two women, but he has his own agenda. Knocking Teyla unconscious, he tries to force Keller to give him the location of Atlantis. Keller discovers that Golan is a Wraith worshipper, and that the Athosians are out there somewhere, still alive. Sheppard arrives and a battle ensues. The team returns to Atlantis, where Keller tells Teyla that she is pregnant.

TEYLA: I brought you here. This is my responsibility. If anything should happen to you...
KELLER: I signed up for this, all right? All of it. I may not have had any idea what I was getting into, but that makes me no different from anybody else on Atlantis.

Writing 'Missing' had been one of Carl Binder's particular desires for season four. Having pitched the idea of Teyla's visit to her people, he was more than happy to take on the task of writing the episode. One of the planned themes of the season was to put Teyla in a darker place than she had previously been, and 'Missing' was to be an important milestone in that journey. Binder was mid-way through the episode when actress Rachel Luttrell revealed that she was pregnant.

Opposite: Teyla tries to reassure an anxious Jennifer Keller.

"I had written an outline and I was in the process of writing a script," he explains. "I hadn't turned in my first draft yet, when she came up to Joe and Paul to tell them.

They immediately told me to stop and come in to see them. So we all sat down and worked out what we were going to do. The thing about 'Missing' was that it really didn't require a whole lot to be done differently as far as taking her in a dark direction went, because as soon as she discovers her people are missing she's going to go very dark anyway. She doesn't know yet that she's pregnant, so it allowed me to still explore that side of it. I just had to add the whole backstory that there was one guy that she was looking forward to going to see. We had to put in play that she had had a relationship with one of the Athosians."

The episode also gave viewers — and the writer — a chance to get to grips with the character of Jennifer Keller. 'Missing' is the first episode in which the character begins to open up slightly, and Binder really enjoyed having the opportunity to add more depth to Keller.

"I really wanted to explore the characters. I thought this would be a good way to pair them up and do a little *Thelma & Louise* episode, and get some backstory about who Keller is and where she comes from. We talked broadly when Martin introduced her in 'First Strike'. Then when I sat down to write her in this, I thought, well okay, here's what I think it ought to be. So I went in and pitched how I saw the character's backstory — small town America, wonder kid. Everybody agreed that would be a good way to go and then I was allowed to explore that much more."

TEYLA: You told them about Atlantis?!
KELLER: No! I gave them a gate address — an uninhabited planet — just to throw them off, buy us more time, like you said.

Exploring Keller's character also allowed viewers to see a slightly different side of Teyla, who is far more usually seen in this sort of situation with the men of Atlantis, rather than another woman.

"Teyla becomes a stabilizing presence as far as getting Keller through this," the writer explains. "It was an exploration of somebody who was a total fish out of water, had never been through this experience, never knew she had the ability to cope in this kind of situation. For me the key scene was when they are both held captive in this little cage, and Teyla sees that she's coming unglued and starts asking her questions about where she's from. She starts getting her to connect to her backstory and uses that as a way to help her find strength to carry on. It was a good way of showing Teyla saying, 'This is what you do to survive.'"

'Missing' was directed by Andy Mikita, who struggled with the logistics of an episode filmed almost entirely on location. "The lion's share of the episode took place outside," Mikita recalls. "Whenever you're shooting outside and on location, you try to keep the trucks close to wherever you're going to be shooting so you don't have to

Above: Teyla, doing what she does best.

lose a great deal of time moving equipment. You want to keep your tools as close by as you can. But one of the areas where we were shooting, with the rope bridge and where they fall down the hill, took place fairly deep in the woods. We had to carry a lot of our equipment, so that was tricky. Plus it's a public park, and we had to work very closely with the parks people to allow us to film in particular areas so we wouldn't be disturbing the natural landscape."

The rope bridge itself was no mean feat to achieve, either. "One of the biggest things was the construction of the rope bridge," Mikita agrees. "That was a big logistical and costly event because we had to build that ourselves, obviously, and there were safety considerations that we had to deal with. Not just for ourselves during shooting, but because it was a park, we had to keep security there twenty-four-seven, basically from the time we started building it and any time we weren't using it, to the moment it was taken down."

Something that Mikita didn't have to worry about was directing new cast member Jewel Staite. "It was not the first time I'd worked with Jewel," the director reveals. "I had worked with her once before when she was in prosthetics as the Wraith in 'Instinct'. So nobody would have known her as being Jewel, of course, because she had been in make-up the whole time, but that was the first time I had worked with her. So when I got to work with her on 'Missing', we already had an established relationship working together, which was great. It wasn't like we had to feel each other out, we already knew each other. Jewel is terrific, and we got along just fine. It was so much fun working with her as the new character, as Dr Keller."

"Jewel's just such a total pro," agrees Carl Binder. "She's a real joy to have on the show." Å

Location Information

Capilano Canyon, North Vancouver.
Latimer Lake, South Surrey.

THE SEER

WRITTEN BY: Alan
McCullough
DIRECTED BY: Andy Mikita

GUEST CAST: Christopher Heyerdahl ([Todd] the Wraith),
Robert Picardo (Richard Woolsey), Jewel Staite (Dr Jennifer
Keller), Chuck Campbell (Technician), Kimberley Warnat
(Linara), Martin Jarvis (Davos)

The team visit a people called the Vedeenan, whose leader can apparently foretell the future. Teyla wants to see if he can reveal anything about her people. Meanwhile, Richard Woolsey of the IOA arrives in the city to give Carter her three-month evaluation. Carter's attention is distracted, however, when a message arrives through the gate that a Wraith wants to meet with Colonel Sheppard. The team arrive at the Vedeenan settlement to discover that the people were expecting them, thanks to Davos, the seer. He demonstrates his skills, but he's ill and Keller diagnoses him as suffering with lymphatic cancer. Carter tells the doctor to bring him back to Atlantis for treatment. Meanwhile, Sheppard meets with the Wraith [from season three's 'Common Ground'] against Woolsey's advice. Of course it is a trap, but Sheppard was prepared — two cloaked jumpers allow him to capture the Wraith and return with him to the city. The Wraith wants to know the base code for the Replicators. They must be reprogrammed, he says, because they are wiping out the Wraith's food supply — humans. Davos shows Carter a future in which the Replicators wipe out Atlantis, but Woolsey insists they must not trust the Wraith. A hive ship approaches, which their captive says is loyal to him and contains the code necessary for McKay to begin his work. A second hive appears, and the Wraith says the city must cloak to keep its existence secret. But doing so will leave them vulnerable. Carter visits the dying Davos, who tells her that though he has never been wrong, his visions can be misinterpreted because he never knows the context. She decides to trust their captive Wraith against Woolsey's express advice, and they cloak. The hives battle each other, ignoring Atlantis, and are destroyed. Meanwhile, Davos, who could not predict his own end, passes away in Keller's care.

CARTER: Mr Woolsey! How was your trip?
WOOLSEY: Well, spending a day in quarantine on the Midway Station wasn't exactly my idea of a good time, but I suppose it beats a three-week journey on the *Daedalus*.

Opposite: Richard Woolsey
(Robert Picardo) isn't
about to give Colonel
Carter an easy ride.

"That one evolved considerably from the time it was originally pitched to the time I wrote it to what actually made it to the screen," reveals writer Alan McCullough. "We broke the first eight or nine stories of season four in the previous fall. So I actually

wrote the script for 'The Seer' before I wrote the script for 'Tabula Rasa'. Originally, it was much more of a self-contained one-off story where Woolsey came to Atlantis and Carter had her leadership review. Then we find this seer and he predicts ships arriving in Atlantis. But it had nothing to do with the Wraith-Replicator war."

Having written the script so early — long before the season actually began to roll — the production team returned from the winter hiatus to discover that many of their plans had to change. "When we came back for season four, we found out about Rachel Luttrell's pregnancy and we had to work that into the season," says the writer. "So the Athosians being missing, that informed the story, and then we learned about the Wraith-Replicator war. Some of the things in the story just didn't work, and so it underwent fairly substantial revisions, both my own second draft and, later, Paul [Mullie] did a draft that changed the story considerably."

The rewrite by one of the show runners is not unusual — in fact, it's worth pointing out that season four was McCullough's first experience of writing for *Stargate: Atlantis*. Although he'd been part of the *Stargate* universe for several years, he had previously only written for *Stargate SG-1*. So although he knew all the characters and had contributed to the show in a general way, he had never before sat down to write a full episode.

"I wrote for *SG-1*, so I knew Carter very well, but all the other characters were very new to me. It was a bit of a trial by fire," he explains. "Nevertheless, I really was proud of what hit the screen. I think it's a very good story, and a great show for Carter and for Sheppard. I think the two of them had great chemistry in that episode."

RONON: That's it? That's the super weapon?
McKAY: What were you expecting?
RONON: Big gun. Something that goes boom.

"I love episodes that have strong multiple storylines," says director Andy Mikita. "Any time some of them can weave together it's great. That particular episode offered a lot of variety, which is always a fun thing to look for in an episode, as a director. It's the opportunity to do lots of different things and not just spend too much time on dialogue sequences. It had a nice bit of action and exterior work as well."

One of the chances the director had to introduce a different approach came with Woolsey's arrival in the city. "At the beginning of act one, Woolsey's character comes through the Stargate and he's talking to Carter on the way up. We did that as just one long steadycam shot," Mikita reveals. "We had the steadycam on a crane, and we had the operator step on to the crane as the guys were walking up the stairs, [then] the crane arm went up and we took a section of railing off the balcony and had grips standing by to escort the camera operator off the crane. He stepped off on to the upper level as Carter and Woolsey walked towards him, and then walked with them into

Carter's office and then back into the control room again. It was fun to choreograph a fairly long running shot, which we don't tend to do too often on the show."

Mikita also had to work on a way to distinguish the seer's revelations from the real-time scenes. Doing so would add clarity for the audience and also gave the director an opportunity to add to the sense of foreboding. Rather than do this in post-production with a visual effect, Mikita decided to accomplish as much as possible at the time of shooting. "We did some in-camera special effects, for the look in the forest and when we were doing flashbacks. The effects that you see in terms of the speed of the camera and when folks were coming in and out of the visions, all those little transition effects that we did were done in-camera."

The visions also caused Alan McCullough considerable stress as he wrote the script, the redraft of which came on the heels of 'Tabula Rasa', which had been another twister of an episode. "We were concerned about how to show those visions," McCullough admits. "It's a tricky one because you have to show the right visions before, and then show them coming true but leave out pieces of information so you're not getting the whole picture. It's the same thing with time-travel stories. It's always trouble to make the present conform to the future or vice versa." He laughs at the memory. "That was my first three months on the show, and I had two tough ones in a row!" Å

MILLER'S CROSSING

WRITTEN BY: Martin Gero
DIRECTED BY: Andy Mikita

GUEST CAST: Gary Jones (Chief Master Sergeant Walter Harriman), Christopher Heyerdahl ([Todd] the Wraith), David Nykl (Dr Radek Zelenka), Mark Gash (Doctor), Kate Hewlett (Jeannie Miller), Sheri Noel (Scientist), Peter Flemming (Agent Malcolm Barrett), Steven Culp (Henry Wallace), Brendan Gall (Kaleb Miller), Madison Bell (Madison Miller), Doron Bell (Sergeant Fuller), Libby Osler (Sharon Wallace), Ron Blecker (Goon)

After helping Rodney with yet another science problem, Jeannie is kidnapped at gunpoint in the middle of the night. McKay returns to Earth to help in the search, only to find himself captured as well. They are being held by Henry Wallace, president of a medical technology company that handles contracts for the government, including integrating alien technology acquired by the SGC into Earth systems, and as a result he knows about the Stargate program and McKay. He wants them to heal his daughter Sharon, who is suffering from leukemia. She has been injected with prototype nanites, but they are having the opposite effect to what he hoped. Their base code needs to be rewritten, and the McKay siblings are the closest thing to experts. McKay refuses to help, out of principle and arguing that they're a long way from being able to rewrite the code anyway. To force McKay to help, Wallace injects Jeannie with the same nanites. If Rodney wants to save his sister, he'll have to rewrite the code. Quickly. Sharon dies before they solve the problem, but then her heart starts up again. The nanites detected a previously unknown heart condition, and shut it down while they repaired it. But doing so cut off oxygen to her brain, and she's now in a vegetative state. Jeannie has epilepsy, and the nanites will do the same to her very soon. Sheppard and Ronon finally find Wallace's lab and arrest him. Sharon dies and McKay realizes he can't rewrite the code in time. He asks their captive Wraith to help, convincing him that doing so would help in the fight against the Replicators. However, the Wraith is too malnourished to work, so McKay offers himself as food. Sheppard intervenes and convinces the guilt-wracked Wallace to step in instead. Jeannie is saved, and able to return to her life.

Opposite: Henry Wallace (Steven Culp) finds a way to make the McKays cooperate.

McKAY: I'm really sorry about all of this.
JEANNIE: Oh, I'm going to hold this over your head for... forever. Like, you're going to eat a lot of vegetarian food and not complain about it.

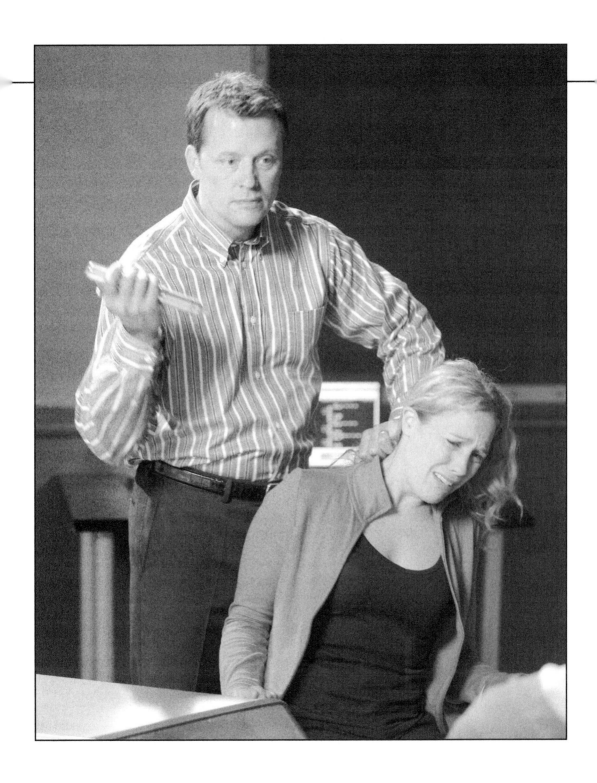

"I wish I had nobler aspirations than just wanting to have a really good time," laughs Martin Gero of why he wrote 'Miller's Crossing', "but I really do love those people. It would be a really good excuse to get everybody in the same city again to go out for some dinners — which never ends up happening because we're always too busy on the show... But 'McKay and Mrs Miller' is probably my favorite episode of the ones I've done myself, it's the one that resonates the most. What I liked about that story was having McKay really have to change his idea of himself through this alternate McKay. And what I liked about 'Miller's Crossing' was the idea that in the first half of the story McKay is very against what this guy is doing. Only when he injects Jeannie with the nanites does McKay seriously consider helping him. And then he's in the same position not twenty-four hours later, when he's standing in front of that Wraith. It's basically a big role reversal to get to the point where he's considering killing himself to help save his sister."

RONON: I look dumb.
SHEPPARD: It helps you blend in a little.
RONON: I'm going to stand out no matter what you dress me in.
SHEPPARD: That's a good point.

'Miller's Crossing' is very different to the episode in which McKay's genius sister, Jeannie, was introduced. Instead of a straight-out comedy episode, Jeannie's return was very action-oriented, which even the writer hadn't anticipated. "That episode turned out way more dramatic than I had intended it to," Gero admits, "so there's not as much of that fun stuff that 'McKay and Mrs Miller' had."

It was also unexpected for actress Kate Hewlett, who reprised the role of Jeannie alongside her real-life brother David. "I really like the character, so I knew that it would be great," she says. "But when I read it, I was really excited! And yeah, a bit surprised, because it's less about family relations. It's a very dramatic situation. It still has those emotional moments, and it still has the banter between them, but it was great for me because I got to be involved in the action side of things, which I've never done before."

"It was funny," recalls director Andy Mikita with a chuckle, "because I didn't even realize. She never really came out and said, 'I've never done action, I've never been around when guns are going off,' and that sort of thing. So I think it was kind of shocking for her, the amount of preparation it would take to do silly little things, like blowing out a door or our guys bursting in to save the day. And those things are *loud*. Having to wear ear protection, that's always a little bit of a tricky thing. When you've got a special effect [exploding] and then you're going right into dialogue, it's really

Above: Ronon, Sheppard and McKay search for clues.

hard for the guys to act properly with earplugs in. You have to at least get started — you wouldn't run a whole scene with earplugs in, but you would want the shot that has the special effect in it to carry on as long as you can before you're forced to cut away. And it was very funny because with Kate having the earplugs in, she wasn't sure when the cues were coming."

"Everything's very safe," says Kate Hewlett, "but they warn you that there's going to be a loud bang. I was like 'Yeah! I can handle this!' My line was the first line after the explosion. So the bang happened — and it was so loud! I was wearing earplugs, and I thought I wouldn't be able to hear anything. But it was *so* loud, and I kind of jumped a little bit and then just froze. The line was mine, and there was this awkward pause… and then I said my line and then the scene carried on. When we'd finished, David went, 'What happened? What went wrong? Who was that?' I was like 'Um… It was me, sorry. But it was *really* loud!' So it was pretty crazy but it was exciting. They must have no eardrums left!"

Martin Gero was particularly happy with the finished episode, and also praises Chris Heyerdahl, who returned to his role as Atlantis's captive Wraith. "I think it turned out really, really well," he says. "It felt very organic to the season, that we would solve a problem based on stuff that we had gotten [previously]. The only way we could get out of that is because we had a Wraith, which happened in 'The Seer', and because of this and that. It really felt like the storyline was coming to a boil there." Å

THIS MORTAL COIL

STORY BY: Brad Wright and Joseph Mallozzi & Paul Mullie
TELEPLAY BY: Joseph Mallozzi & Paul Mullie
DIRECTED BY: William Waring

GUEST CAST: Kavan Smith (Major Evan Lorne). Chuck Campbell (Technician). Jewel Staite (Dr Jennifer Keller). David Nykl (Dr Radek Zelenka). Torri Higginson (Dr Elizabeth Weir). Sean Millington (Marine). Ernie Jackson (Replicator). Reese Alexander (Major Jordan). Tammy Hui (Replicator Gate Tech)

The gate hasn't worked for a week, and McKay and Zelenka are trying to work out why as a probe hits the city. It's covered in nanites, and McKay is convinced the Replicators have found them. The probe explodes before he can examine it further, and McKay is suspicious — something just feels off. Later as Sheppard and Ronon spar, the warrior says he also feels that something is odd — people are acting differently. Sheppard takes a hit and goes to the infirmary for stitches, but Keller can't find a wound. She reluctantly scans him for nanites, but says she can't see anything. Sheppard demands a blood test. Later, Lorne and Keller meet and discuss some sort of shady mission, and Lorne reveals he destroyed the probe. Sheppard doesn't trust Keller and runs tests on himself, Teyla, Ronon and McKay, discovering that they're all infected with nanites. Moreover, according to the computer there are no other life signs on Atlantis except them — and one other. Ronon and McKay locate it and discover Elizabeth Weir. Keller arrives and explains that this Atlantis and everyone in it are Replicators — and Sheppard's team are clones. These Replicators have split from Oberoth and are trying to ascend by studying the cloned team, whose memories will now be wiped. Oberoth's Replicators have found the dissenters, however, and attack. Weir convinces Keller to let them out to fight Oberoth, and she gives them the coordinates of all his ships. They contact the real Atlantis and give them the information, but the Replicators track them. To allow the 'real' team to escape, the clones create a distraction, sacrificing their lives to give Atlantis a chance.

McKAY: I did not break the gate.
SHEPPARD: It just happened to stop working about the same time you were screwing around with it.

'This Mortal Coil' began the huge wrap-up that was *Stargate: Atlantis*'s mid-season four two-parter. Right at the beginning of discussions about what they wanted to see for the year, the producers and writers had decided that it was time to bid the Replicators farewell.

"The Wraith, who were our 'big bad' in seasons one and two, had kind of fallen into the background as we shifted focus over to the human form Replicators," explains

Opposite: Elizabeth Weir's clone tries to reason with Sheppard.

Above: The team think they've found a friend.

Joseph Mallozzi. "And the Replicators are interesting, but I find the Wraith infinitely *more* interesting."

Having two major bad guys in one show seemed like overkill for the writer, and so in discussion with the rest of the team, he decided that one of them had to go. In finding a way to do just that, Mallozzi came up with the clone idea, which would later also be used to bring back Dr Beckett. This gave Mallozzi an opportunity to play with the audience, who for the first half of the episode have no idea that the characters they are following aren't the actual team. It also gave him a chance to explore something that he personally enjoys.

"I always loved the idea of the 'other' you," he explains, "having your characters meet themselves, and that's kind of what we wanted to do with this particular episode. It just explores, on a philosophical level, what makes you you. At the end of the day, these individuals at the beginning of the episode *are* the team. They're not the originals, but in every other way they are the team, and so at the end of the episode it was actually kind of touching, and a little depressing, to see them realise that they have to sacrifice their lives for this alternate team who, as far as they are concerned, are just as much them as they are."

The episode also answered the question of just what happened to Elizabeth Weir after the events of 'Lifeline'. Sadly, the doctor met a tragic end, as the original Weir was already long dead by the time of 'This Mortal Coil'. But it did allow the producers to ask actress Torri Higginson to reprise her role. Though Higginson was happy to visit the set again, she admits that the idea of playing a different version of the character was a little perplexing.

"Well, that whole episode was strange," she laughs. "Everyone kept saying, 'Hey, am I a Replicator? What exactly am I? They told us that we weren't actually Replicators, we were clones. But to be honest it was a hard thing to grasp. It was such a finite distinction to make. I think it was more difficult for the other actors than for me, because there was only one of me at that point, and she knew that. There was no ego grappling with her at that moment."

SHEPPARD: You doing OK?
WEIR: Sure, all things considered. Not bad for a dead woman.

For Mallozzi, the episode couldn't quite live up to the idea behind it, simply because the mechanism of the story required such a lot of explanation. "To be honest with you, looking back at it, some things worked and some things didn't," he says candidly. "The problem with this particular episode is that it required so much exposition that I feel it bogged the episode down. There were some great moments, and it came together well. Torri came in and she did a terrific job for us. It was just the sort of episode it was. At the beginning it was all very interesting, as we're trying to figure out what the mystery is and what's going on. And then, between the end of the second act and the beginning of act four, things slow down as the Replicators explain what the heck has been going on. And you need that, but it's just unfortunate. Once that's done, and we get into our real team going to meet them, then things really pick up again and the episode ends with a bang. I don't think there's anything I would have changed, per se — it's just the type of story that was being told. There's really nothing you can do. And of course 'This Mortal Coil' set up 'Be All My Sins Remember'd', which is a huge free-for-all — one of the biggest episodes we've ever done. I thought 'This Mortal Coil' did a fine job of setting it up, and then we all really hit it out of the park." Å

BE ALL MY SINS REMEMBER'D

WRITTEN BY: Martin Gero
DIRECTED BY: Andy Mikita

GUEST CAST: Michael Beach (Colonel Abe Ellis), David Nykl (Dr Radek Zelenka), Christopher Heyerdahl ([Todd] the Wraith (Voice)), Mitch Pileggi (Colonel Steven Caldwell), Torri Higginson (Dr Elizabeth Weir), Chuck Campbell (Technician), Niall Matter (Lieutenant Kemp), Jill Wagner (Larrin), Martin Christopher (Major Kevin Marks), Brendan Penny ([Todd] the Wraith), Michelle Morgan (FRAN)

The evacuation of the planets in the Replicators' path is almost complete, but some settlements refuse to move. Caldwell and Ellis arrive with the *Daedalus* and the *Apollo*, ready for use now that they have a way of tracking the Replicator ships. McKay wants to use the Replicator destruct code he has been working on with the Wraith, but it's not ready. The colonels decide to go with the military option, and the battleships move out. A week later, Caldwell returns to the city and is told that the Replicators are falling back, obviously unable to work out how they are being tracked. McKay's destruct program still isn't ready for use, but he suggests another idea — issuing a command that makes all the Replicator blocks bond together. They'll eventually adapt, but they should have self-destructed long before then. The device can be beamed into the Replicator homeworld, transmit the necessary code, and that will be it. Unfortunately there will be a delay before the ships orbiting the planet are affected. They need to be destroyed. The Wraith says he may be able to help by bringing more ships to the fight. While McKay works on the Replicator device, Sheppard and the team take the Wraith to rendezvous with a hive. After a slightly hairy few moments for the team, an alliance is formed with seven Wraith hives. They are on their way back to Atlantis when Larrin's ship appears and offers to join the battle. On Atlantis, McKay has made progress and created a female Replicator named FRAN (Friendly Replicator Android). She warns McKay that his plan will fail as it will work too slowly. She suggests that overloading several ZPMs at the site will speed up the process. The battle begins and FRAN is transported to the Replicator homeworld, beginning a chain reaction as she activates her programming. The Replicator blocks fuse into a giant mass which sinks to the planet's core and explodes, destroying the remaining Replicator ships in the shockwave.

Opposite: FRAN (Michelle Morgan), the answer to all of McKay's problems.

CARTER: There's one more thing you need to see. McKay has thrown us kind of a curve ball.
SHEPPARD: Oh great. I was just thinking we need more of those today.

"I get a lot of positive feedback about that episode and I feel quite guilty about it," laughs writer Martin Gero. "People are like 'Why can't you do episodes like that *all the time?*' Well, for one, it was one of our most expensive episodes last year. There were a ton of visual effects. Mark Savela and his team did a spectacular job in some of those battle sequences. But the reason that episode is so satisfying is there are ten episodes leading up to it. All the really exciting stuff in that episode — Teyla's pregnant and that finally comes out, we get to work with Todd, and Larrin comes back, and then there's FRAN and we're finally going to kill the Replicators — that's been a year and a half coming. So it's got a season of momentum behind it, basically, and it's an *end*. Which is hard for us to do in these recurring shows. We kill those guys — those guys are finished. Those are no longer our bad guys."

The visual effects really do stand out as some of the most spectacular ever accomplished for the show. The episode also contained one of the few effects that has ever made visual effects supervisor Mark Savela run a cold sweat. Savela is known for his laid back, relaxed attitude to whatever is thrown at him by the *Stargate: Atlantis* producers. But this time, he thought he'd met his match.

"Probably the scariest thing I've ever seen on paper in a script was 'A giant blob the size of a city'." He says with a laugh, "It's not the easiest thing to accomplish!"

McKAY: Well, I mean, I hate to speculate.
SHEPPARD: Oh? Since when?

"I don't often see Mark Savela scared, or openly nervous," says Gero. "The greatest part about Mark is that he never says no. He's always, 'Yeah, we'll figure out a way to do that,' and he does it with a confidence so you think, 'Alright, I'm sure he will.' With the blob, he was like, 'I… don't know how we're going to do that. I *hope* it turns out.' So I was nervous only because Mark was nervous! I tried to explain it as best I could, and it came out pretty much exactly how I had described it. Somehow he managed to find a cool way to do what I described. But yeah, it was a big blob of Replicator parts in the middle of the city. I don't know what the hell I was thinking when I tried to do that. It sinking into the ground, and having it gel and solidify, and having those shots where millions of particles are flowing through the air — those are super, super complicated shots."

At the other end of the action scale, the episode contained a particularly emotional moment as Teyla finally reveals her pregnancy to Ronon and Sheppard. It's a tense, painful scene, and one that director Andy Mikita worked hard to get right.

"The biggest thing that I had wanted to try to convey was the awkwardness of it all," the director explains, "the awkwardness of Teyla having to finally come out and state the fact that she was pregnant, and how Sheppard was going to deal with it. I thought Joe did a good job of that one — the fact that he was obviously still caring

Classified Information ▶

In the shot where Ronon walks Teyla off-camera after she reveals her pregnancy, actor Jason Momoa took advantage of having his back to the camera and ad libbed several lines and jokes as he walked away. None of them made it into the final cut for obvious reasons, but the cast and crew had to struggle to keep a straight face...

for her and her wellbeing, and it manifested itself by him getting very, very angry and taking her off active duty right away. He was using the excuse of all the other people that she could potentially put into danger, but the reality was that he cared about her."

To convey that sense of discomfort, Mikita collaborated closely with the three actors he was working with — Rachel Luttrell, Joe Flanigan and Jason Momoa — prior to shooting.

"I thought it was going to take us a lot longer to shoot that scene, and ironically it took no time at all," he recalls. "Rehearsal fell together very quickly. I kept the staging very loose, just to see how it would play out in a natural way. I didn't give very specific direction, like, 'You're coming here and you're coming here.' All I staged was having the two groups coming together and then seeing how it played out. The big thing was the distance that Teyla was going to be away from him when she made the initial statement that she was pregnant and then moving in closer. Everybody was on the same page. And I thought Jason did a terrific job, showing Ronon's care for Teyla, and the way he walked her out of the scene was really quite nice." Å

SPOILS OF WAR

WRITTEN BY: Alan McCullough
DIRECTED BY: William Waring

GUEST CAST: Christopher Heyerdahl [Todd the Wraith [Voice]], Andee Frizzell [Wraith Queen], Scott Heindl [Male Wraith], Kavan Smith [Major Evan Lorne], David Nykl [Dr Radek Zelenka], Brendan Penny [Todd the Wraith], Morris Chapdelaine [Newborn Wraith]

The team detects an apparently abandoned Wraith destroyer, which Sheppard decides to investigate. He leaves Teyla behind, worried about her pregnancy, but when they discover that it's a derelict with no Wraith aboard, he asks her to help them fly it. She agrees, but on the journey Ronon activates a map that McKay believes reveals the location of a Wraith outpost possibly housing technology that allowed them to defeat the Ancients. Teyla manages to fly to the coordinates, but is severely weakened. The team leave her on the ship as they investigate. The outpost holds a Wraith Queen in suspended animation, and they observe a Wraith being birthed from a pod suffused with the Queen's DNA. But there are thousands of pods — one Queen couldn't supply DNA for all of them. Discovering that the Wraith, dubbed "Todd", is being held prisoner, the team free him and he explains that only a handful of Wraith descend directly from the Queen. The rest are cloned — which is how they defeated the Ancients ten thousand years ago. Todd reveals that he took the ZPMs from the Asuran homeworld to power the facility, and was then betrayed. The team go to retrieve them, but are captured in the attempt. Teyla tries to distract the Queen by connecting to her mentally, and she manages to free Sheppard, Ronon and McKay. They get back to their Wraith ship and escape in a puddle-jumper, allowing the destroyer to crash into and obliterate the cloning facility.

McKAY: Don't worry, I've got an excellent sense of direction.
SHEPPARD: Didn't you say you got lost in a garden maze once?
McKAY: I was ten, plus I was running from a bee!

'Spoils of War' was another example of the darker turn that the show had taken — and another curve in the arc that the season was following. According to writer Alan McCullough, the episode was important for the set-up of the season finale, which was already in the minds of the producers.

"We hadn't written the script yet, but we knew essentially that Teyla was going to be kidnapped by Michael and we would attempt to rescue her and be unable to

Opposite: Sheppard and Ronon contemplate an untimely end.

because that was how the season was going to end," he explains. "So we knew that somewhere along the line we had to feed in the fact that the Wraith had cloning technology, because we had never said that. So, knowing those things, I tried to come up with a story that dealt with Teyla a little bit, but also seeded the cloning technology into Wraith mythology so that we could eventually use it to bring back Beckett."

One of the most striking scenes of the episode is the conversation between Teyla and the Wraith Queen, played by Andee Frizzell. McCullough reveals that this wasn't in his original storyline, and came out of a need to have a representation of what was going on between the two in Teyla's head. "Someone came up with the idea of just focusing on Teyla and then having the Queen appear behind her head and talk, jumping from side to side behind her head, which worked beautifully. Will Waring shot that very well."

"He's such an amazing director," agrees Andee Frizzell, who has played every Wraith Queen since the series began. "He trusts in his actors to do what they're supposed to do. When we walked in he just said, 'Okay, here's the scene, here's where the camera's going to be, go to it.' I was drawing from that Hannibal Lecter-style mind torment. Will just allowed the camera to swivel from side to side to pick me up, and he gave me all of the artistic freedom to do it how I had envisioned. And Rachel is so receptive — she reacted physically to my voice."

Classified Information ▶

Actress Andee Frizzell has to re-record every line of her dialogue in ADR (additional dialogue recording) for every episode she films as the Wraith Queen • because the teeth give her a lisp!

McKAY: You touched something, didn't you?
RONON: No... Maybe just a little.

Whenever the Wraith are on screen, and particularly when an episode is taking the viewer inside their environments, the look of the production is paramount. Season four gave fans a chance to see a lot more of the Wraith 'at home', so to speak, which was a challenge for the art department because, in reality, *Stargate: Atlantis* has only one standing set dedicated to the Wraith.

"The other production challenge was making the ship look different from the facility," agrees McCullough, "because of course it was the same set! But I think they did a great job of that, too. You're very clear what location you're in."

For production designer James Robbins, 'Spoils of War' was a chance to establish more of the Wraith infrastructure that had been hinted at in the series but not seen. "We had two episodes that were very heavy in the Wraith set and we did a lot of revamping of the interiors," explains Robbins, "creating a new environment in there as well as building some new physical pieces. In this particular episode the cloning pods were the real new thing. We actually built three different pods with various stages of cloned growth inside, and of course the last stage was with a live actor, who was in the process of being 'birthed'. It was all wonderfully horrible and gooey!"

This glimpse at the method that the Wraith use to reproduce added an extra element of horror to an already horrific foe. It wasn't something that has been addressed in the series before, and McCullough says that it was another important story point that the writers felt it was time to reveal.

"We had all discussed how the Wraith reproduced," he explains. "We hadn't locked into anything, but I remember years ago when we talked about it, Rob Cooper thought that it took place in a ship. The Queen went into a pod and her DNA went into the ship and it seeded other pods. But of course that's another thing we've never actually said! We've all talked about it in the room but it's never actually been seen, so we had to somehow find a way to hook that into the scripts."

Above: McKay learns more about the Wraith from Todd (Brendan Penny).

Though they had the basic idea of how the Queen seeded the ship, the details of what the process would look like were still fluid. In discussions with Robbins and Mark Savela of the visual effects department, it was decided that the apparatus should be physical, and the idea of the chair took shape.

"I had done a rendering of the Queen in her chair," says Robbins. "What I'd done in my drawing was less wardrobe and more part of her environment. But it was a little too revealing for an episodic show! So [costume designer] Val [Halverson] adapted what I had drawn into a physical costume that she could wear. When she stands up, the elements of the materials that she used in the costume are very much in keeping with the whole Wraith feel. It was very organic and using this sort of bat-wing material. All the effects that we used were represented there. I thought Val did an absolutely wonderful job."

The art department also had to build the physical parts of the chair that would connect to the Queen once she was seated. "We built some physical pieces to attach to her and changed out the Wraith throne that we'd used in the past. When our actress came in, we did a fitting with her and laid these pieces over her arms so it looks like she's literally melded into the chair. Then visual effects added a whole bunch more, so that she is able to retract these things. With the help of VFX they all just sucked back into the chair."

For the writer, 'Spoils of War' is ultimately a chance to explore a story that stretches back millennia, and he was very pleased with how it turned out. "I love the story," Alan McCullough confesses. "I also love that we find out just a little bit more about the Wraith-Ancient war from 10,000 years ago: how they were able to clone warriors to defeat the Ancients. I love pulling things out of the past and bringing them to light. When I'm searching for stories, I look at what happened in the past and think, well, *how* did that happen?" Å

QUARANTINE

WRITTEN BY: Carl Binder
DIRECTED BY: Martin Wood

GUEST CAST: Brenda James (Dr Katie Brown), Chuck Campbell (Technician), Kavan Smith (Major Evan Lorne), Jewel Staite (Dr Jennifer Keller), David Nykl (Dr Radek Zelenka), Sharon Taylor (Amelia Banks)

McKay reveals to Sheppard that he's going to propose to Katie Brown. However, as he arrives in the botany lab, Atlantis goes into lockdown. No one can move around the city. Carter finds herself stuck in a transporter room with Zelenka, Sheppard and Teyla are locked in McKay's lab, Ronon is in the infirmary with Keller, and McKay discovers that Katie's laboratory has no computers and no way to communicate with the rest of the city. But he knows that a lockdown has to mean that a pathogen has entered Atlantis. Sheppard remembers McKay's password, and he and Teyla begin to work out what's happened. Sheppard realizes there is no pathogen, but the city is broadcasting a distress call into deep space — and it can only be shut down from the control room. He breaks out of McKay's window and climbs the tower, but doing so sends the city into self-destruct mode, as it thinks the pathogen has proliferated. Meanwhile, Katie has discovered the engagement ring, but McKay says there's no longer any point in proposing as he can feel himself getting sick. Ronon tries to blast through the infirmary door, but fails. Sheppard realizes the only way to shut down the self-destruct is to reboot the city completely, but they've got to get to the power room and they have limited amounts of C-4. They retrieve Carter and Zelenka, who suggest using the ventilation system. Zelenka crawls through the ducts and manages to shut down all systems in time. Normality is resumed and the doors open — just as Ronon and Keller are about to share a kiss. Meanwhile, McKay realizes he's not ready for marriage and he and Katie call a rain-check on lunch — and possibly their whole relationship.

CARTER: We could really use one of your pigeons around now.
ZELENKA: They're not for eating!

In case you hadn't noticed, *Stargate: Atlantis*'s fourth year has some pretty big episodes. 'Adrift', 'Be All My Sins Remembered', 'Midway', to name but three. Stories like these make for extremely large budgets, and somehow the show needed to think smaller. And that's how the funny and touching 'Quarantine' came about.

"We needed to do a small episode," explains writer Carl Binder, "so we talked around various ideas about a contained episode on Atlantis. I think it was Joe Mallozzi that came up with the idea of isolating various people in parts of the city. As soon as

Opposite: Carter and Zelenka have the chance to get to know each other better.

he said that, I jumped all over it. I love the small episodes. I love the character pieces, and I saw this as potential to have a lot of fun with a lot of pairings. We just needed the mechanism to get them all isolated, and then it just became a matter of who gets stuck with whom and what we can play out from that. I was really excited."

Instead of going for the 'obvious' pairings — for example, having Carter and McKay stuck together as an opportunity for their trademark bickering — Binder wanted to mix things up a little. "I thought it might be fun to have Carter get stuck with Zelenka, who's kind of like McKay's rival," Binder laughs. "That's an unusual pair. We hadn't really seen them do any scenes together, so how would that dynamic play out? I played it that Zelenka has always had this secret crush that he would never ever in a million years admit to. That's sort of the undercurrent playing throughout their whole story."

'Quarantine' also gave viewers a chance to learn a little more about new arrival Jennifer Keller's background, which had not been explored. Putting the petite doctor with the imposing figure of Ronon Dex yielded some surprising results.

"I can't remember who thought of the idea of Ronon and Keller together," Binder says. "But as soon as I heard that I thought, 'That's a great idea!' Then we had Teyla and Sheppard together, because at that time we were working on 'Be All My Sins Remember'd' and also 'Spoils of War', which was the whole relationship playing out with regards to her baby and her place in the team. So that felt like a good fit to explore that some more."

KELLER: You tore your stitches. Honestly, I've never met anyone with such reckless aggression. That's not a compliment.
RONON: If you say so.

Classified Information

The vent set that Zelenka crawls through was actually made of plywood, since metal would have been too noisy. The clanging sounds as Radek moved around were added in during post-production.

Another very significant pairing was that of McKay and Katie Brown, the horticulturalist that the scientist had been quietly dating since season two. The producers felt that something had to be done to move the relationship forward one way or another.

"We'd planned all season that McKay would propose to Katie at some point and then that would end up not coming to fruition, so we decided this would be the perfect episode to put it in to. 'Quarantine' was a real writing staff group effort as far as molding the various pairings and the storyline went," explains Binder. "Then it was just up to me to go off and write the script."

Binder's enthusiasm for the story meant that he was looking forward to sitting down and spinning out the dialogue between the pairings the producers had chosen. The pairing that the writer found most difficult was the one that, ironically, he had the most freedom with — Keller and Ronon. The idea of seeing the two of them together in conversation was so new that finding a starting point, particularly for Keller, who had as yet had little screen time, was a challenge.

"We hadn't really seen them interact or play off each other at all, and I wondered how they would, and where they would find some common ground between them," he explains. "So I worked my way to this place of each of them putting the blame on themselves for things that have happened in their lives. They each have a moment where they say to each other, 'It's not your fault.' They let each other off the hook — Ronon blames himself for what happened on Sateda and she feels like she's not doing her job in Atlantis."

Though most of the action takes place within the city itself, Binder felt that at some point being stuck inside small rooms with these characters would become too claustrophobic to be a satisfying episode. Having Sheppard climb the tower became the answer, leading not only to the resolution of the quarantine problem but also a chance to see Atlantis from a very different angle.

"I realized that Sheppard isn't going to sit still," explains the writer. "He's going to do whatever he can to get out of that room to figure out what's going on. So maybe he figures out how to get the door open, but then he's in the corridor and we're still inside. I needed to get outside, and that's when I thought, 'What about a free climb up the side of the tower?' It was something I'd never seen, and we've been trying to get a better feel for just how big this city really is. So what I thought would be great was a helicopter shot of Sheppard climbing the side of the city, and since that's the only big visual effects sequence in the entire episode, we'd still be a small episode. I was thrilled, especially with the high angle looking down. That was a shot that Martin Wood put in there that I hadn't originally envisioned, and I thought that was a great idea."

The exterior climb by Sheppard called for James Robbins to work his magic on a new set. "We had to make some physical changes to McKay's lab," says the designer. "Fortunately for us, the McKay lab set actually has a window that leads to an area that plays as part of an exterior pier. So all we did was revamp the exterior walls. We made the window a little bit smaller and had Sheppard start his walk right from there. I went online and found a lot of images of elements that climbers run into on climbs, and tried to incorporate those into the architecture of the exterior of the tower. Although we've seen the tower a lot, we'd never seen it up close in detail so that you could see what the surface was like and where you could get a handhold. We built a twenty-foot wall section and we also had some changeouts so that it could play for forty feet of wall. It was gimbled so that it would angle and make the climb easier if it needed to be."

As it turned out, however, actor Joe Flanigan had absolutely no qualms about the wall that Robbins wanted to create. "Flanigan has some history of doing rock climbing," Robbins reveals. "So we didn't worry about making it easy for him — quite the contrary. We simplified the build so it would be a bit more difficult to climb. He went out that window and up that wall like a monkey!" Å

Above: John Sheppard sees Atlantis from an entirely new perspective.

HARMONY

WRITTEN BY: Martin Gero
DIRECTED BY: William
Waring

GUEST CAST: Crystal Lowe (Mardola), Jerry Penacoli (Genii Warrior), Jodelle Ferland (Harmony), Patrick Gilmore (Genii Soldier), Alexis Kellum Creer (Flora), David Richmond•Peck (Genii Field Captain), Richard Stroh (Genii Soldier), Adam Lolacher (Genii Man)

On a trading trip, Sheppard and McKay agree to help two princesses with their sister, Harmony. She is destined to be queen, but must first complete a pilgrimage, which they do not want her to do alone. The two men agree, and then discover that, in fact, she's a kid. A very annoying, very insistent kid. The pilgrimage means a trek through the forest to some sacred ruins, taking an ancient pendant worn by Harmony that is supposed to tell if a future queen is worthy of the role. They set off, McKay and Harmony bickering incessantly. However, the trio soon hear a noise that Harmony identifies as a fearsome beast that roams the forest, but she's not scared and insists on continuing. Sheppard suddenly vanishes, and a group of Genii men surround and capture McKay and Harmony. Sheppard launches an ambush and frees them, and Harmony says that her mother banished the Genii. Sheppard realizes someone at the palace must be working with them. He wants to return, but Harmony refuses and runs off. They eventually find her, and she asks Sheppard to be her king. They hear screams and Sheppard investigates, finding two dead Genii apparently savaged by the beast. He overhears their leader ordering the search for Harmony to continue. Sheppard again insists that they get Harmony out of there, but she refuses — they are close to the ruins. Sheppard stuns the Genii guards, and McKay realizes it's an Ancient device and the pendant activates it. The 'beast' is in fact the sound of mini-drones. The Genii have scrambled the crystals, but McKay says he can fix it. Harmony argues that she can make it work with the pendant, it's her birthright as queen. As the Genii attack, Sheppard uses the pendant to activate the device and fight off the men. Later, back at the palace, it is discovered that one of Harmony's sisters, jealous of Harmony's selection as queen, hired the Genii to stop her being crowned.

HARMONY: Provide me with cover. I will make it to the pedestal, summon the beast, and smite them.
SHEPPARD: There will be no smiting today, little lady!

The *Stargate* franchise has a history of turning out excellent comedy episodes, and 'Harmony' certainly qualifies. Written by Martin Gero, the episode takes the 'fish out of water' approach and applies it to the two characters least equipped to deal with small children — Sheppard and McKay.

Opposite: The Genii's latest dastardly plan is thwarted.

"It was a fun episode, and it goes back to one of my favorite things in this show and that's the Sheppard-McKay banter," says David Hewlett. "I love that. And I think Sheppard is in his environment when he's in the woods and he's got his guns and he's got to take the lead and stuff. He's basically looking after his two kids — Harmony and McKay!"

Working with children is reputed to be difficult, but child star Jodelle Ferland had so impressed the producers with her turn as the young Adria in *Stargate SG-1* episode 'Flesh and Blood' that Martin Gero specifically wrote 'Harmony' for her.

"I would never have written it if we couldn't have had the girl that we had," he explains, "so before I even started writing we booked Jodelle. I feel like we didn't really burn her out in *SG-1*. She played such a small role, but it was such a great, memorable one. So that's how it started. We're writers *and* producers here, so whenever I have a good idea I have to think three weeks down the line to when the script is going to be finished and how I'm going to produce it. A lot of the time you'll do something as a writer that really shoots yourself in the foot as a producer. It's kind of like slapping your future self in the face," Gero chuckles ruefully. In this case, it was the casting that would have caused the problems. "Because in television you don't have an enormous amount of time to cast. And if you write a huge part for an eleven year-old, and then you don't find an eleven year-old that week, you're screwed and the episode will be very bad."

Ferland herself was very happy to return to Bridge Studios. "I thought it was going to be probably one of the most fun roles to play," she says. "I always get to play scary roles. And in this one, I'm a nice little girl — I'm a mean little girl, but at least I'm not scary! I like being mean in movies. It's fun. And they're the most amazing costumes I've ever had," she exclaims. "When you go for the first time, they're basically putting material on you to see which ones go well, and it's so neat to think that they make it all themselves, the dresses and everything. I had a lot of fun on both of them."

Classified Information

This script originally featured Ronon as well as Sheppard and McKay. Jason Momoa eventually had to be written out to accommodate filming on 'Outcast' and 'Quarantine'. which partially overlapped with 'Harmony'. But that's what sequels are for!

HARMONY: When the Genii started firing at me, you threw yourself on me, using your own body as a shield.
McKAY: Oh no, no, no, no, no! I just, I just tripped and fell on top of you. It was an accident.

The young woman also had no problem with keeping the *Stargate: Atlantis* cast and crew in line either, much to Hewlett's amusement — and consternation.

"She is the most scarily perfect actress ever," says the actor. "I've never met anyone who knows her lines that well. She not only knew *her* lines, she was correcting me on mine. It was fun, because I teased the hell out of her. I'm merciless with children, because I don't believe that they should get any special treatment. One of the fun things that I've been able to add to the McKay character is his complete and utter

disregard for children," Hewlett laughs. "I love those characters that begrudgingly like kids. But we say kid — she's such an adult. Honestly, I've never met anyone that technically good. She hit her marks, she was always ready… She may have screwed up her lines twice — and I killed her for it. I did not make it easy for the poor girl, and she was fantastic! I was smart enough not to get into the swearing thing that everyone got into, though. If they swore they'd give her money, and I refused to be a part of that because I could see that she was a shark. She must have walked off the set with hundreds of dollars!"

"With these episodes it's always kind of a leap of faith," Gero confesses. "You're writing an episode that rests all of its success on the shoulders of an eleven year-old girl. That's a terrifying thing to do. Also, we were shooting out in the middle of nowhere. There were some great vistas that we don't usually get, especially at the beginning of the episode, because we drove an hour and a half outside of Vancouver. So it was just a very difficult episode to produce. And so when you sit there in the editing room and you see it all play back, that's always very rewarding. I really love the scenes between her and Sheppard in the cave, and her and McKay, when she's asking what love feels like. Because you don't want her to be wholly awful. She's a spoiled brat, but she's also very cunning and smart. I think that episode turned out quite well." Å

OUTCAST

BASED ON AN EPISODE
CONCEPT BY: Joe Flanigan
WRITTEN BY: Alan
McCullough
DIRECTED BY: Andy Mikita

GUEST CAST: Dean Marshall (Sergeant Bates, USAF Retired), Bill Dow (Dr Bill Lee), Kari Wuhrer (Nancy), Emma Lahana (Ava Dixon), Stephen E. Miller (Dr Richard Poole), Dylan Neal (Dave Sheppard), Adrian Hein (Replicator), Kwesi Ameyaw (Tactical Sergeant), Ayesha Shiva (Woman)

Sheppard returns home for his father's funeral accompanied by Ronon. At the wake, Sheppard is reunited with his ex-wife, Nancy, but the proceedings are interrupted by a woman called Ava Dixon, who catches Sheppard's attention by knowing things she shouldn't. Ava reveals that she works with a Dr Richard Poole, and that they managed to build a Replicator. Three weeks previously, it went on the run and they can't find it. Ava thinks they need help. Sheppard arrests Poole, who refuses to comply until Sheppard threatens to arrest Ava. Having narrowed down the search area, they locate the Replicator, and Poole tries to talk it into deactivating itself. His arguments fail, and he pays with his life. The Replicator escapes, and Sheppard asks Nancy to help by using her government contacts. Poole must have had a buyer for the technology he was developing. Nancy refuses. Then they discover that the real Ava has been dead for a year — the Ava they met is also a Replicator. They go to retrieve her but she's vanished. Nancy changes her mind after looking at Sheppard's file and realizing that whatever he's involved in must be serious. Her information leads them to a warehouse where the Replicator is hiding out. They try to take it down, but fail. Sheppard is saved only when Ava arrives and the two Replicators slug it out. She distracts the male Replicator long enough for him to be beamed into low orbit, where he burns up on re-entry. Ava is captured, and her body destroyed — though her consciousness is released into a virtual Earth, where she is told she must never work in the sciences again.

RONON: So, what do we do now?
SHEPPARD: Well, mostly people sit around, drink, eat... Some more than others. But mostly they talk. They don't know what to say, but they talk.

'Outcast' came out of an original concept pitched to the producers by series star Joe Flanigan, who liked the idea of seeing the *Atlantis* character in an Earth-based setting.

"He had pitched the idea of a Replicator on Earth," says Alan McCullough, who ultimately ended up writing the screenplay. "We liked the idea of that and ran with it. We were trying to spin the story, and for years we have been getting fan requests to get a little more of John Sheppard's backstory. We knew about a lot of the other

Opposite: Sheppard reassures an oblivious Ava Dixon (Emma Lahana).

characters, but Sheppard was an enigma, so we thought maybe we could pair that up with the story. In the first place, the easiest way to get him back to Earth was a death in his family. And it seemed like a good opportunity to explore a little more of his history."

Though the death of Sheppard's father formed an excellent plot mechanism for putting the character back on Earth, it also threatened to unbalance McCullough's script.

"It was another challenging script," says the writer. "We were dealing with things that were new territories for the character. We had never seen Sheppard dealing with loss — we had lost Weir and other characters, but there was something very personal about getting this glimpse into his life. It was a bit of a challenge to write and to get the tone of that right. The tendency was to go too far. Faced with that grief, how much would he say and what would he talk about? Also, once the Replicator story takes over, it is such a powerful draw that it pulls away from the other story. We almost forget about the death of the father, because we're caught up in the Replicator being loose on Earth. It was a challenge to make sure we didn't just abandon the death. That would inform your behavior for the entire episode, no matter what you are doing. I actually thought Joe Flanigan did a great job. He's always a great actor, but in that particular episode he shone. That was a tough acting challenge, I think — to not get caught up in the action and still have that memory of your father's death at the forefront of your mind."

RONON: I watched it last night. There was hardly any fighting.
SHEPPARD: It's not about fighting.
RONON: Then why's it called *Blades of Glory*?

Another particularly memorable aspect of the episode are the locations where it was shot. The viewers discover that Sheppard comes from a particularly affluent background, and the locations department scouted a beautiful area of Vancouver for the occasion.

"We've got a wonderful locations department here," says director Andy Mikita. "They had come up with this house in the Southlands area of Vancouver, and it was one that had just come onto the market in terms of being used as a filming location. Kudos to them for finding it as quickly as they did. We're always prepping so quickly, and it was great that they were able to find it in such short order. There're not a lot of places like that for filming, so it was wonderful to get a place where we were allowed to photograph outside for basically anything we wanted, wherever we wanted. We tried to incorporate the stables and to give it the air of old-school money that he would have come from, which is something that viewers were not expecting."

Another location was the industrial area where the chase happens, culminating in the Replicator's leap from a huge crane. Filmed at the B.C. Sugar Refinery, the

location department was able to get the production excellent access to shoot on and around the site. This meant that Andy Mikita could set up some fabulous sequences for stuntman and actor Adrian Hein, who was hired to play the Replicator. As a member of the Vancouver Freerunners Society, which practices the art of parkour (an athletic movement dedicated to using only the human body to move from one object to another), Hein had no qualms about creating an amazing daredevil sequence worthy of a Replicator.

Above: Freerunner Adrian Hein performs a gravity-defying move.

"He was sensational," says McCullough. "We had to hire a stuntman to play the role because there were so many stunts. So he's more professionally known as a stuntman, but he's also an actor. He did a great job of portraying the robot 'emotions' of a guy who's betrayed and is now on the run and is desperate. But the parkour was a big part of his casting too. The first time we did a location scout to check out the crane, he came with us just to see if he was comfortable climbing it. We were there looking at it and he just started doing this parkour thing up the side. It was amazing. He was up the entire crane in about six seconds! No one could believe how fast he could move. That brought a lot to the episode, to have a guy that was able to do that."

Ironically though, when it came to the giant leap from the top of the crane, Mikita had to bring in a stuntman for the stuntman! The plunge into the water was actually performed by *Stargate: Atlantis*'s stunt coordinator James Bamford. Hein could have done it himself, but had he been injured in the process (however unlikely), the production would have ground to a halt with their guest star out of commission.

"Whereas BamBam, he's expendable," Mikita jokes. "So we tossed him off the top. It was a one shot deal. It was kind of tough for him, because it takes a long time just to get the cameras and the boats into position so that it all works out okay. Meanwhile, he's up there preparing himself to make the jump, but it actually takes a good hour and a half to two hours of preparation down on the ground before we're ready to pull the trigger. It was kind of a shame, because we ran several cameras, I think five, and one of them didn't run. There was a technical problem with the camera so it was an unusable shot, which was a pity. It would have been a really cool one. But as it turns out I think we only used three of the angles anyway." Å

TRIO

WRITTEN BY: Martin Gero
DIRECTED BY: Martin Wood

GUEST CAST: Jewel Staite (Dr Jennifer Keller), Isaah Brown (Caminous), Aidan Drummond (Renord), Nico Ghisi (Kid), Alberto Ghisi (Kid)

Carter accompanies Keller and McKay to M5V-801. They need to convince the population to move, as they are all suffering from respiratory problems as a result of being forced to mine an unknown substance by the Genii some years previously. As they approach the village, McKay plunges into a hole — swiftly followed by Carter and Keller. It's an abandoned mining facility. Prying a door open, they discover they are suspended in a huge shaft with only stilts holding the room up. They've got to find a way out before their combined weight causes it to collapse. The only way is up and out through the hole through which they fell. First, they try constructing a pile of crates which Carter climbs — but it collapses. A group of children find them, but refuse to go for help as they're forbidden to be in this area for this very reason. A tremor shakes the room, tilting it further into the chasm. Very soon they'll be out of time. The trio try throwing grappling hooks through the hole, but there's nothing for it to sink into above ground. They try to build a bridge based on Keller's memory of an old bar trick with three beams, but another quake makes it collapse and Sam falls, breaking her leg. Another quake causes the room to pitch even further and Keller falls out of the door, only saved by a rope held by McKay. Carter can't move to help hold her, but as McKay starts to pull her up, Keller spies light — there's another way out. McKay has to lower her and Carter down before following himself, and almost gives up until Keller talks him through. He makes it to the second mineshaft as the room pitches into the chasm. Much to McKay's surprise, Keller later invites him out for a drink.

McKAY: It's not going to scar is it?
KELLER: Chicks dig scars.
McKAY: Not the chicks I dig.

"I always spend too much money on my episodes," confesses writer Martin Gero, "and I was hoping to do a cheap show. So I thought, 'I'll put those three guys in a room. How expensive can it get?'"

The answer is, pretty darn expensive. What Gero had intended as a low-budget story shot in one set spiraled into one of the most complicated and costly episodes of the season. In theory, the fact that the production would be re-using a set originally built for the *Stargate SG-1* movie *Continuum* should have eliminated most of the costs.

Opposite: McKay, Keller and Carter find themselves in serious trouble.

But as the episode took shape, the producers realized that the set — already one of the most elaborate ever produced for the franchise — required more adaptation than originally thought.

"We decided we wanted the room to tilt more, which was a huge deal," the writer explains. "It tilts 150 percent more than it did in *Continuum*, and it's this big three tonne steel room — you can't just move it around. Then we couldn't figure out how to get them out of the room. When we decided that, there was a $150,000 set that we had to build. So what is essentially three people talking in a room became impossibly complex!"

It wasn't just the logistics of making the script work that was difficult, either. Gero reveals that actually working out what should go into the script — which was of a very different style to anything he'd written for the show before — was a challenge in itself.

"It's a difficult script, period, because it is essentially a one-act play. It takes place in one set for the entire episode, and they're all geniuses down there," he laughs, "so even the ideas that they come up with that fail have to still be pretty good ideas! Just coming up with the ins and outs of why those plans were going to fail and ultimately how they were going to get out and have it be a satisfying thing was difficult. And then, of course, you have to come up with dialogue. I tried to build in work times so that while they were doing the work they could be talking, because it never felt right to just have them sitting down there talking. They're in trouble, and they needed to be doing something about it. So as long as they were actively working towards a plan, I could have them talking about whatever I wanted."

KELLER: I see light!
McKAY: No! No, no, no, no! Don't go toward the light! You want to stay in the land of the living!

Filming brought its own issues, particularly for stunt coordinator James Bamford, who had to work out how to rig all the boxes to fall in precisely the right place on a set that was at times hard to stand straight in.

"It was very cramped, and getting in and out of there with the film crew and still keeping safe was difficult," he says. "I had a full safety crew there every single day, and my usual wire riggers also hired extra safety riggers for the crew. It became very difficult to move around in there, and very claustrophobic. It was also very odd once the set began to tilt for certain scenes. Some crew members got really nauseous at eight degrees. When it was tilted at twenty-two degrees, everybody was standing on an angle and people were slipping. It was quite a challenge, that set."

"It was absolute HELL to shoot," agrees David Hewlett. "But it completely conforms to my theory that the worse things are to shoot, the better they are to watch.

Above: McKay checks on an injured Samantha Carter.

I should probably walk around with a stone in my shoe all the time or something, because it just leads to better acting. It was hell to shoot, but that said, I was with Amanda Tapping and Jewel Staite, two of the female icons of sci-fi geekdom," he adds gleefully. "No nerd in their true mind would complain about being stuck in a room with those two. Both of them are wickedly funny, and I mean *wicked*. They are terrible. They get me going and I start laughing. We must have wasted so much videotape just cracking up. We had this whole musical number worked out for a theatre version of *Stargate* that we were going to do once we all got fired because of this episode. We had so much fun doing it."

Once he had begun writing, Gero had been very concerned that the episode would end up being short, since working out how long the scenes would take to run was very difficult.

"An average episode that I write has, like, a hundred scenes," he says. "This had ten. So it was really hard to gauge how long the episode was going to be. And I know that when David gets talking sometimes we just race through it! I did overwrite it a bit, just to protect us. It was also going to be next to impossible to re-shoot scenes, because we were slowly destroying the set. It was shot completely in sequence, and it would be very difficult to go back to a certain point."

In fact, the finished episode was so far over that the writer had to hack back many scenes — and lost one entirely. "It was too bad, because it was one of my favorite exchanges," he says, "where Sam hints very heavily that she's involved with O'Neill. It also kind of talked about where Keller is with the whole Ronon situation. But it was an extra minute in an already slow part of the episode, and it really would have done irreparable harm to the pace."

Gero feels that the cutbacks, along with Martin Wood's direction and the performances of Hewlett, Tapping and Staite, helped make 'Trio' a great episode.

"They are an extraordinary group of performers," he says. "They had days where they had ten or fifteen pages that they just ripped through. And Martin shot it so brilliantly with these long takes, so they would get full attacks on the scenes. It was really something to watch." Å

MIDWAY

WRITTEN BY: Carl Binder
DIRECTED BY: Andy Mikita

GUEST CAST: Bill Dow (Dr Bill Lee), Gary Jones (Chief Master Sergeant Walter Harriman), Ben Cotton (Dr Kavanagh), Chuck Campbell (Technician), Scott Heindl (Wraith Leader), Christopher Judge (Teal'c), Toren Atkinson (Dempster), Nickolas Baric (Hester), James Chutter (Wraith Scientist), Rob LaBelle (Mr Coolidge), Brendan Penny (Wraith Technician)

Ronon has to face the IOA review board and Carter, worried that he may not present himself in the best light, asks Teal'c to give the young warrior some pointers. Ronon is not best pleased and does his utmost to ignore the former Jaffa, until their shared ire results in an almighty sparring match, watched by the crew. The day comes for Ronon and Teal'c to journey to Earth through the Midway Station, where they will have to remain in a twenty-four-hour quarantine — and share quarters. A group of Wraith have learned of the station's existence and launch an attack. Taking Dr Lee and Dr Kavanagh hostage, they demand they be given passage to Earth. Their interrogations do not work, but they are still able to open a gate to the SGC, with an active IDC. They send a device through the gate to Stargate Command, knocking everyone there unconscious. On Atlantis, they have realized what's wrong but can't get to Midway, because of the outgoing wormhole. The Wraith enter the SGC without resistance, followed by Ronon and Teal'c. As soon as they can, Sheppard and his team gate in to Midway and engage the remaining Wraith, but are unable to retake the control room. More Wraith begin to gate in, and Sheppard tries to find a way to disable the gate. On Earth, Ronon and Teal'c find Coolidge, the IOA member charged with assessing Ronon's suitability. He insists they call for reinforcements, but the two warriors refuse, saying they have it under control. Sheppard orders McKay, Kavanagh and Lee to evacuate to a puddle-jumper and blows all the air out of the station to kill the Wraith, surviving by means of a space suit. The fight for the SGC goes on, and Teal'c and Ronon finally prevail — together. Later, the IOA gives Ronon the all clear, grateful for his valor.

TEAL'C: Indeed.
RONON: You say that a lot.
TEAL'C: What?
RONON: "Indeed".
TEAL'C: Do I?
RONON: Yeah.
TEAL'C: I had not noticed.

Opposite: Ronon and Teal'c (Christopher Judge) — together on screen at last!

"It was a big episode," writer Carl Binder says with a laugh, remembering how 'Midway' came together. "Paul Mullie was terrified of this episode, he kept saying, 'We can't do this, we can't do this…' but at a certain point we realized we *had* to do it and then he just said, 'Well, in for a penny, in for a pound!' It was always going to be a big episode, which is why we had to do episodes like 'Quarantine' and 'Harmony', some of those smaller episodes, in order to be able to do the bigger ones. Especially since we knew the whole Midway gateroom was a virtual set. We had to create that entire set, so that was a huge deal."

The episode was huge in every sense: the sets, the fights, the visual effects — and the casting, which is really what got every fan's attention as soon as it was announced. Because 'Midway' saw, finally, the meeting of Ronon and Teal'c, as actor Christopher Judge reprised his much-loved role from *Stargate SG-1*.

"I just loved the idea of he and Ronon playing off each other," says Binder. "Ronon is kind of the unwieldy puppy who needs to be shown how to behave. You have these two warriors, both of whom have been through a lot of battles, but the one has the wisdom of many many years, and the other is a young hot-head. I loved the idea of getting those two together."

Classified Information

The gateroom in the Midway Station is actually the gateroom from *Stargate SG-1*. Green screens were used to block out everything except the gate and the ramp.

RONON: I'm exactly the kind of team member they want out there fighting the Wraith. Their words, not mine.
TEAL'C: And you did not hold a weapon to their heads?
RONON: I did not.
TEAL'C: I am pleased.

Of course, a massive part of the episode was the chance, not only to see these two characters together, but to see the action that would ensue as they fought — both each other, and side by side. It was something that stunt coordinator James Bamford was more than happy to choreograph. One of the most spectacular fight sequences was the sparring scene when the two go head to head — literally.

"The sparring match was shot in a different way," Bamford (more widely known as "BamBam" on set) explains. "Andy Mikita saw it in a specific way, the way it was written, being seen through the crowd as opposed to actually getting right in and seeing the fight. In actual fact, it's not as long as it appears to be. All the intercuts make it seem longer than it is. There were so many things going on, the betting of the spectators, the dialogue between Sheppard and Carter, and then the fighting itself and what was going on in the fight. We wanted to capture the one-upmanship between Ronon and Teal'c, to try to get a sense of the new replacing the old and the 'I'm going to teach you little boy' attitude. So I tried to get that in there."

Binder confesses that at first he wasn't sure that the scene was going to play out

as he'd originally intended. "I left it up to James Bamford but we did discuss it in the production meetings as to what we wanted from it. It's interesting because on the day, I went down there just to watch the rehearsal while they were practicing it, and then I had to go back up to the office. When I saw it all edited together, especially when Carter comes in to interrupt the scene, it was playing much too serious for me. I'd always envisioned her jumping into the middle of it, trying to break them up, she can't break them up, they go back at it again, she finally breaks them up... I just wanted it to be a little more of a boys-will-be-boys kind of feel, and she's the mother coming in to break up the boys from fighting. But they were playing it really dead serious. So I spent a lot of time in the editing room crafting it together, cutting to the crowd cheering and to them going 'Oooh' when she breaks it up. And also cutting to Joe Flanigan a lot, because he was the one character who was actually playing the whole sequence lighter, so by cutting to him frequently I was able to lighten the tone of the scene. So it took a little work in the editing room, but in the end I was very happy with how it came out."

Above: Sheppard realizes the gravity of the situation.

'Midway' was, ironically considering the episode's outcome, the first time viewers had properly seen inside the finished Midway Station.

"It went through various stages of size," the writer explains, "in that the first time we saw the completed station, in 'Adrift', it felt a little small to me because this station has to be big enough for a puddle-jumper to fly out of one gate and into the next. So that gateroom had to be fairly large. Then you have the crew manning the station, and they have to have quarters to sleep in. So I tried to play off that, and make the guest quarters very cramped, which adds to the fun of Ronon and Teal'c having to share a room." He laughs, adding, "But it did come off as a little bit bigger than maybe we had intended." Å

THE KINDRED

WRITTEN BY: Joseph Mallozzi & Paul Mullie
DIRECTED BY: Peter F. Woeste

GUEST CAST: Jewel Staite (Dr Jennifer Keller), Paul McGillion (Dr Carson Beckett), Mitch Pileggi (Colonel Steven Caldwell), Kavan Smith (Major Evan Lorne), Connor Trinneer (Michael Kenmore), Christopher Heyerdahl (Todd the Wraith), Heather Doerksen (Major Meyers), Chuck Campbell (Technician), Patrick Sabongui (Kanaan), Artine Brown (Trader), David Beairsto (Merchant), B.J. Harrison (Female Merchant), John Sampson (Human Guard), Igor Hudacek Jr (Scavenger)

Teyla dreams that she is watching the funeral pyre of her child's father, Kanaan, and wakes convinced that he is trying to contact her. Meanwhile, Keller tells Carter that a plague is spreading through the galaxy, wiping out human populations on many worlds. Teyla has another vivid dream, where Kanaan shows her a pendant she bought him. Carter authorizes a mission to the planet where Teyla acquired it as Keller works on the disease. She discovers that it is mutated from the Hoffan virus created to destroy the Wraith. Teyla finds a merchant selling the pendant she saw in her dream, along with other items owned by people she knows. He says he found them in a fresh grave and Teyla insists on being taken there, but a Wraith dart suddenly appears and abducts Teyla. Todd the Wraith reveals that they are also dying from the disease, and offers to tell them who created it if they help find a cure — but only for his hive. Teyla finds herself Michael's captive, and discovers that he took the Athosians. He has experimented on them, turning them into hybrids. Michael wants Teyla's child, which possesses a special gift, and reveals that he has Kanaan captive too. He is a hybrid, and under Michael's influence. Sheppard's team arrives aboard the *Daedalus*, which is attacked by a hive as they search the facility. A Wraith tells them the prisoner is aboard the ship, and Sheppard tells Caldwell not to destroy it. It escapes as the team discover a guarded cell. Killing the guards, they open it to discover something they didn't expect — Dr Carson Beckett.

McKAY: So, it's just a matter of time before they become hungry and cranky!... Well, I mean, I know I would.

'The Kindred, Part 1' was directed by Peter Woeste. Although he had been part of the *Stargate* universe for a long time, Woeste had never previously helmed an episode of *Stargate: Atlantis*.

"It was a big challenge for me," he confesses. "Although the two series were connected at the hip, I was really involved on the *Stargate SG-1* side. I didn't have any

Opposite: The long-awaited return of Dr Carson Beckett.

background in *Atlantis*, and I have to admit I hadn't seen any of the episodes. I had seen the pilot, but I wasn't following it. So when they asked me to direct it, I thought, 'Oh my god, now I have to learn backstory from three seasons!' *Atlantis*, like *SG-1*, was used to directors who had been involved year after year and had done multiple episodes, so they were really part of the process. To go in as somebody new, I felt a little intimidated."

Despite his trepidation, Woeste's experience as a cinematographer and director — a history that stretches over twenty years and includes documentary, movie and television making — stood him in good stead. By bringing the director on board, the producers were opening the show to the potentials of a new eye. It was a chance for Woeste to present a fresh approach to a show that had been shooting for three and a half years.

"That's what everyone was counting on," agrees the director, "and I tried to do that. The cast were fantastic. They were all very welcoming. Whenever I could I would say, 'Well guys, you tell me. You're the regulars,' and they would be so helpful. I just can't say enough about those guys. Whenever I got stuck, they would help me out!"

SHEPPARD: That's not going to happen.
TODD: You always say that. But you always come around.

Besides the worries of being a director that didn't know the shorthand that any long-running cast and crew develops, Woeste also had logistical challenges to overcome. One occurred during his attempt to shoot the opening teaser sequence, in which Teyla dreams of Kanaan's funeral pyre. "When we shot that, it was summer and things were very dry," Woeste recalls. "The location was in the middle of Surrey, B.C., a little park there, and the local fire department said that we couldn't actually have an open fire. There were obvious problems with that and all sorts of things were talked about. We said, 'Well, maybe we can just use flame bars in front of the lenses, or we can try to do it in post.'"

Neither option worked for the director, since realistic fire is hard to achieve with anything but a practical effect. Moreover, James Robbins, whose art department had built the pyre, had specifically designed the prop to be as safe as possible. "We had to reassure them that the actual pyre build itself had been fire-proofed and nothing in it would burn," says Robbins. "It's a controlled propane thing, and it only looks like it's burning. I think N. John Smith, one of our executive producers, stepped in and chatted with the fire department and got them to see reason. So we were able to do that on location."

Being able to use a location to shoot was a huge relief, since it was completely impractical for the production to shoot the scene at Bridge Studios, where the greens department would have to bring in an entire forest of greenery to achieve the location called for in the script. Even so, the fire department's solution still created difficulties for Woeste.

"They pointed to an area where they said maybe I could have a very small fire. But the problem was, it was at the edge of a parking lot," he laughs. "There was only one little grouping of trees that I could use as a background because everything else was parking lot and gravel pit. So shooting that scene, the set was one 'wall' — that little wall of trees. We shot in one direction and then turned everything around. The cameras didn't move, but the actors would come on the other side and we'd cheat their point of view. So that was a difficult one!"

Woeste also had to pull a few cheats out of his hat when filming in the set produced to be Michael's laboratory. The facility needed to look large, but James Robbins only had a limited amount of space on which to build.

"That was a set that was at our Norco stages," says the production designer. "There wasn't a whole lot going on in there except a little bit of a firefight. They wanted Earth-based architecture, which made it a little more straightforward for me. So we went in, and we had an existing set that had played in *Continuum* on that stage. I tore down parts and put up some new walls to create the rooms they required — one room for the fight with the hybrids and the other where they find Beckett at the end of the episode."

"It had been the temple where Ba'al is executed," says Woeste, who was director of photography on *Continuum*. "It started as that. It was cut in half and they added four pillars that we could move around. So I moved those pillars in every way I could! I had people coming from behind and going through and passing by… We had some set dressing that we would move around, to create this huge underground facility that they were searching and having firefights in."

What the director was most pleased with, however, has nothing to do with raging funeral pyres or firefights. His favorite scenes of the episode are far smaller scenes.

"I was most pleased with the scenes between Michael and Rachel," he reveals. "I love the performances. Over the years on a series there is continuity, the characters are formed — it's very difficult to inject anything new. You try to, and that's probably why I enjoyed those scenes between Connor and Rachel, because that's something that is me, and I could work with their performances." Å

THE KINDRED, PART 2

WRITTEN BY: Alan McCullough
DIRECTED BY: Martin Wood

GUEST CAST: Christopher Heyerdahl (Halling), Linda Ko (Marie), Paul McGillion (Dr Carson Beckett), Jewel Staite (Dr Jennifer Keller), Connor Trinneer (Michael Kenmore), Patrick Sabongui (Kanaan), Ken Kirzinger (Bartender), Mark Curtin (Guard), Mylene Dinh-Robic (Anika), Johann Helf (Nabel Golan)

Taking Beckett back to Atlantis, the team discover he's a clone. The doctor doesn't know this — as far as he's concerned, he was kidnapped by Michael during the events of 'Misbegotten' and has been waiting for rescue ever since. McKay has to explain everything that has happened since that point — including Beckett's own death. Meanwhile, Michael leaves Teyla in a cell with the remaining non-hybrid Athosians — including her friend Halling. In an effort to prove he can be trusted, Beckett gives them the coordinates of a planet to investigate, but they are attacked by Nabel Golan, whom Keller first met on New Athos. They take him back to Atlantis, where Beckett collapses. His system is shutting down, and needs a drug, which Michael was evidently administering. Teyla sees Kanaan again, and tries to get through his hybrid programming. Their child's life is at stake. He begins to recognize her, but Michael interrupts and the moment is lost. Sheppard questions Nabel, and offers to help him if he does the same for them. Eventually he tells them the coordinates of Michael's base. Beckett insists on accompanying the team, though his condition is getting worse. Michael detects them as soon as they arrive and orders his hybrids to kill them while he escapes with Teyla. The team rescues the Athosians, but gets into a firefight. Beckett finds Teyla, who can't believe her eyes, and won't leave without Kanaan. Michael appears and Beckett is unable to shoot him — his clone programming makes it impossible. Michael takes Teyla. Sheppard and the team can't stop them, and Beckett goes into a steep decline. They return to Atlantis without Teyla. Keller says that Beckett must go into stasis if he's to have any chance of survival.

BECKETT: My god. They're dead.
McKAY: You think Teyla...
SHEPPARD: No, I don't think so, and you don't think so.

At last it was time for what many fans had been waiting more than a year for — the return of Dr Carson Beckett! Despite being killed off in the season three episode 'Sunday', we all know that no one ever really dies in science fiction — and 'The Kindred, Part 2' was proof of exactly that.

Opposite: Teyla tries to get through Kanaan's hybrid programming.

THE KINDRED, PART 2

"Joe Mallozzi contacted me and asked me if I'd be interested in coming back to the show," says actor Paul McGillion. "He told me the circumstances and it sounded really interesting. I'd had such a great time on the show for three years, and I loved the idea of going back."

Bringing Beckett back wasn't just a case of creating an appropriate mechanism for him to physically return. Carson's clone — who, to all intents and purposes is the man himself — had to be brought up to speed on everything that had happened in the year since his original died. As is to be expected in the Pegasus Galaxy, that was a lot. It fell to McKay to fill his friend in on what had been going on, which led to a very powerful scene between the two characters. For writer Alan McCullough, who had never written for Beckett before, it was a difficult scene to perfect.

"It was challenging," says the writer. "Partly because he was such a beloved character and this was the first time, apart from a little flash in Joe's episode, that he was back. I wanted that return to be memorable and true to the character. I wanted his reactions to be genuine — there was the news that he had died and he couldn't tell his mother and also that Weir had died — so those were challenging scenes to write. That scene with him and McKay, when I first wrote it, I think it was about seven pages long, and that was no good. I put it into two halves and cut to somewhere else to break it up, but even then it was a pretty weighty scene. It's very rare that you get an opportunity to write such a long scene."

**SHEPPARD: I'm tired of getting shot at with our own guns.
BECKETT: I'm generally not fond of it, regardless of the weapon.**

McCullough may have found it difficult to accomplish, but McGillion in particular was appreciative of his efforts. "I love that kind of writing," says the actor. "I read it and I thought, 'This is some meaty stuff for me to bite into.' I felt it was great for the fans to see that, and I also felt as an actor it was a wonderful opportunity for me to play the emotional core of this character. Put yourself in that situation — your whole life has changed completely and you come back and everybody has moved on. He's being bombarded with all this information and it's his best friend telling him. I thought it was a really powerful scene, very poignant. I think it shows the multi-dimensional layers of the character that the writers have developed over the past three or four seasons. That's a testament to the writing. Brad and Robert gave me a great character to play with and it's great to see him being fleshed out."

For director Martin Wood, the key to making the scene work was to make sure that the audience was not concentrating on anything but what the two characters were

saying. To accomplish this, he duplicated the movement that he had established in a previous episode. "I had set up something in 'Tao of Rodney'," Wood explains. "I wanted this to hark back to that. It was the same room, and the initial shot is very similar. I wanted viewers to be familiar enough with the room that they weren't going to look at it. So I wanted to set it up so that the audience was only dealing with the faces. These two are talking, and nothing else. Don't jump around, no weird angles, don't do a whole bunch of pushes; don't do things that force people to lose the scene, even for a second. Directors do those things in order to enhance something that we think is slow. In a case like this, you realize that it *has* to be slow. It has to allow the time to act out their story. A lot of times, there is as much, if not more drama that happens in a dialogue scene as in an action scene. So it is as exciting for me to go into a really brilliantly written dialogue scene, where I know the actors are going to eat it up. You get some real emotion and you get to actually see acting happen, rather than just them talking. That's very exciting for me."

Above: The team mounts a rescue.

Another scene that the director wanted to emphasize was the closing shot of Beckett being frozen in the stasis pod. The audience is saying goodbye to the character for a second time, and in a much more prolonged way.

"Paul was a huge deal in that episode," he says. "The whole thing at the very end was something that we talked about a lot — how we were going to do it and what we were going to do. I think it was a brilliantly written scene. I really liked the way that Alan brought everyone together. Because you're saying goodbye to somebody while he's standing in front of you and he doesn't leave. For me, as a director, it was a change of pace. In regular television, a person says goodbye and they walk away or we walk away. In this case, it was just seeing him standing there, and we were standing there. I didn't want anyone walking away. So the camera moves away instead. The very last shot is the camera pulling away from him, to give it the same feel you have when someone walks away."

Of the finished episode, McCullough says, "It was tough. I struggled with it. But I was glad with the way it turned out and I think the episode is very strong." Å

THE LAST MAN

WRITTEN BY: Joseph Mallozzi & Paul Mullie
DIRECTED BY: Martin Wood

GUEST CAST: Andee Frizzell (Wraith Queen). Chuck Campbell (Technician). Christopher Heyerdahl (Todd the Wraith). Kavan Smith (Major Evan Lorne). David Nykl (Dr Radek Zelenka). Connor Trinneer (Michael Kenmore). Robert Picardo (Richard Woolsey). Jewel Staite (Dr Jennifer Keller). Heather Doerksen (Lieutenant). Kate Hewlett (Jeannie Miller). Kory Grim (Recruit). Christian Sloan (Hybrid). Dan Kashagama (Doctor)

After following a lead on Teyla, Sheppard returns to Atlantis to find it utterly changed. The city is abandoned, and the planet has become a desert. Trying his radio, Sheppard raises McKay, who tells him to go to the hologram room. There, an aged representative of Rodney tells him that he's been pitched forty-eight thousand years into the future, but he has a way to send him back. Sheppard will have to spend another thousand years in a stasis pod before the right solar event occurs, but sand has blocked the corridors to the stasis room. He'll have to go outside, where a deadly sandstorm is brewing. As they wait for the storm to abate, McKay explains what happened after he was lost to them. The team found Teyla dead, with Michael having taken her baby. He used it to speed up his breeding program and spread the plague. Carter died on a suicide mission. The IOA sent Woolsey to take over, and everything fell apart. Then McKay realizes that the sun will burn out in five hundred years, so Sheppard can't use the stasis pod after all — unless they can use the sun's increased solar corona to provide power to maintain the city's atmosphere. Sheppard soon realises he'll have to fight his way through the sandstorm. As he does, McKay tells him how Ronon died in a raid on one of Michael's labs. Sheppard makes it, and asks what happened to McKay. Rodney tells him he resigned and returned to Earth. Keller did the same when Woolsey wouldn't let her continue treating the plague victims. On the journey home, they fell in love. But Jennifer soon fell ill and died, and McKay spent the rest of his life trying to undo the past. Armed with Teyla's location, Sheppard makes it back to present-day Atlantis and launches a rescue mission. But the building is booby trapped, and collapses on top of them.

McKAY: If I don't get you back within two months of when you left, then it'll be too late.
SHEPPARD: Too late. What the hell's that supposed to mean?

Opposite: John Sheppard gets help from a (very) old friend.

"It was all about the fact that we couldn't shoot Rachel in the twentieth episode," explains writer Paul Mullie, "so we couldn't wrap up the pregnancy storyline. But it had to be big, and if we were going to deal with some other problem and then come

back and deal with her problem, it was going to be this weird interlude and it wouldn't have worked well as a finale episode. I needed to do an episode that dealt with the problem without her being in it. So the idea of doing a time travel story, where in the future the Rachel storyline has been wrapped up in a certain way and then you can come back and do it over again, suddenly fit. The new element you have gained as a result of having been to the future is the knowledge of where she was being kept. It suddenly made sense to do a time travel story."

One of the major aspects of the episode is the aged figure of Rodney McKay. Like a character out of a Greek tragedy, the doctor finds himself witness to the gradual dissolution and destruction of the Atlantis team. Actor David Hewlett was required to undergo several hours of prosthetics to achieve the required effect, and says he had great fun doing so.

"I'm an old school film nerd of the *Evil Dead* genre," Hewlett says, "so when people start sticking stuff on people's faces, I love that. It's actually incredibly comfortable, because you basically come in for four hours in the morning and you sit there and someone just plays with your face! That puts me to sleep in seconds. I tried to talk them into a bald cap. I was like, 'There's no way McKay would have hair — look at him!' But thank god they didn't because that just would have been horrible. My only thing is that of course, like McKay, I have the most sensitive skin in the world. But what was neat was, I *did* walk around like an old man. In fact, someone said to me, 'Wow, that's amazing, the prosthetics, and then what, there's some sort of padding thing they're doing too?'" The actor laughs. "I was like, 'No! There's no padding!' But it was fun. You just let everything go. You don't stand up straight — everything that bothers me in my body I got to play up: my knees, my back, my neck hurting. What I discovered in that show was that I was born to be old. Some people were born to be free, some people were born to ride... I was born to age!'"

McKAY: Sheppard is not dead.
WOOLSEY: Right. He's just been transported forty-eight thousand years into the future. I guess that makes him one of the lucky ones.

For director Martin Wood, one of the most enjoyable parts of the episode was filming the sandstorm that Sheppard has to struggle through. At first the production had not thought it possible to create the storm physically. But special effects guru Wray Douglas found a way, meaning that Wood could film the scene without computer generated effects. Rather than sand, however, which would not show up adequately on screen, Douglas used cornmeal. Lots and lots of cornmeal.

"BamBam [stunt coordinator James Bamford] and I went down and stood on the set in front of the big wind machine. Then Wray started to throw this cornmeal into

Above: Rodney McKay will do anything to turn back time.

the fan, and we could kind of feel it but it wasn't so bad. It didn't hurt the way that sand would sting," explains Wood. "So we stacked up the fans — there was one shooting past the cameras and then there was one shooting at the actor so the close-up camera would be on him. I had three cameras running, and there was one on the actor's face the whole time. When we started, the door opens up and BamBam came out. He did it about six times. Then Joe walked in and said, 'Okay, I'll do it.' He put his kerchief round his face, put his glasses on, and did it four times. So you see a lot of Joe in that scene. BamBam only did it a couple of times.

"Yeah, the clean-up on that was a good one," Wood chuckles. "I didn't have anything to do with that!"

"It was one of those ones I was worried about very much," confesses Hewlett. "But then I sat down and watched it. I'm always amazed by that. You lose so much of these shows by making them. When you are in the scenes they feel so disjointed and you think, 'Was I good in that, was I acting well?' With 'Last Man', I was hoping I'd hit all the right notes, because I talk about Carter dying, but I'm not there and I haven't seen it. You've got to have someone to talk to for that stuff. And Joe just did such a good job of this stoic sadness to all this news, because he just literally had to sit there and listen to me tell him how everybody died," he chuckles. "At one point I think he actually said to me, 'My god, you're depressing!' McKay is just the most depressing person alive... 'And then she *died*, a *miserable* death. Happy, sort of — but *miserable*!'"

"I was proud of that script and I think Martin did a great job," says Mullie. "It just worked. And Joel Goldsmith did an amazing job of scoring that episode — the whole sequence where Carter dies Joel made ten times better with the music. It's one of my favorite scripts I've ever written." Å

COLONEL JOHN SHEPPARD

"Surfing a thirty-foot wave in Waimei is cool. Dating a supermodel is cool. This is not cool!"

Season four saw a lot of upheavals for the character of John Sheppard. First, he was forced to take command when Elizabeth Weir was incapacitated. Then the colonel was charged with welcoming Atlantis's new commander into the fold whilst facing the prospect of his closest friend, Ronon, going his own way with his Satedan compatriots. And if all that wasn't enough, the character also had to do battle with an inversion of himself. All in all, it was a hectic start to a hectic year. So it was perhaps a relief for the actor that the change of show runner from Brad Wright to Joe Mallozzi and Paul Mullie didn't mean any radical differences on set.

"Joe and Paul have been here an awfully long time on *SG-1*," Flanigan points out. "The truth is that our producers don't often come to set. We rarely see them. That's just the way they've set it up. So having new show runners doesn't really affect the day-to-day aspect. What I noticed in the writing is that it appears there are slightly fewer character pieces and more team pieces."

One of the big "character pieces" for Sheppard in year four came very early on. 'Doppelganger' is an interesting episode, and in some ways shows how far the character of John Sheppard has progressed since audiences first met him in the pilot, 'Rising'. For the lead on a show to play an 'evil' version of himself, the character has to be very well established, so rooted and so solid that such a role change doesn't affect the overall reception of the character. And there's no doubt that John Sheppard is about as solid as they come.

"'Doppelganger' was a lot of fun," Flanigan recalls. "That was the first show we shot coming back from hiatus. And Robert Cooper called me at home and wanted to discuss the script. That's what I love about Robert — he gets really excited and he wants to talk to the actors and he wants to go over all this stuff."

The actor had no issue with seeing his character — or at least, a shade of his character — take a turn to the dark side. Antagonists are often said to be more fun to play, and starring as the hero of a team every week doesn't often afford a lead actor that chance.

"It was an exciting project to work on," says the actor. "It was challenging, too. It was exhausting. I actually don't think my shoulder has fully recovered! I had to fight myself and then turn around. Throwing phantom punches is harder than actually hitting a solid object. It takes twice as much energy. And then to turn around and throw another set of phantom punches — because we split-screened everything — it was physically difficult to do."

Later on in the season, viewers got to learn a little more about John Sheppard's background, something that Flanigan has been pushing for since season one. In fact, 'Outcast' came from a story suggested by the actor himself, out of a desire to meld two story elements — an adventure that would require some or all of the team to return to Earth, coupled with a glimpse of Sheppard's past history.

"I thought that it would be nice to go back to Earth," he says, "and in going back to Earth we could discover some backstory for my character. I always thought that if we were going to explore backstory there had to be some connection to what's going on [in the Pegasus Galaxy]. I had this vision of Jason and I running around trying to find a Wraith. My original idea was that a Wraith had come back to Earth. They chose a Replicator, which was the same basic idea. I like Earth-based science fiction, it can be a lot of fun."

As far as the character's backstory went, Flanigan reveals that 'Outcast' held as many surprises for him on that score as it did for the audience as a whole. Fans learned that Sheppard was from an affluent background, and could have stayed there if not for his rebellious streak that saw him more comfortable with military life than riding horses and small talking at dinner parties.

"I definitely had my differences about it," the actor recalls. "That's not what I chose. I chose for my father to be alive, because I pictured my father being an imposing and eccentric figure who could be a very interesting recurring role on the show. I didn't envision Sheppard coming from a wealthy background. So that was just a choice that they made — I think it was kind of *Batman*-esque. And it worked. It doesn't really make any difference, the point is that you learn *something* about him."

Season four saw Sheppard strengthening his bond with Ronon Dex even further. Episodes such as 'Outcast' show how well the two work together, particularly in action situations. Flanigan feels that having such a dynamic is very important, because though at other times it works to have Sheppard teamed with other characters — take 'Harmony', for example, where he interacts mostly with McKay — Ronon and Sheppard are balanced, both physically and mentally.

"We did a lot of stuff together," he agrees. "Before there was a lot of Sheppard-McKay, but now it seems like we do more Sheppard-Ronon stuff, because we're able to do pure action when we're doing that. The reality of McKay and Sheppard chasing Replicators in some high-octane action-fuelled moment is not as plausible. So when Ronon and Sheppard team up we're able to do these pretty cool action episodes, and I'm totally with the action episodes!" Å

PROGRESS REPORT
Colonel John Sheppard

I don't need to tell you that, whatever problems may have once existed in his military career, John Sheppard is an exemplary officer. His mission reports, however briefly written, should be testament to that. His courage and dedication to duty in the face of extreme adversity is of the sort that I have rarely encountered before. As I write this, I am faced with the possibility that he is lost to us forever, alongside several other of my command team who are all equally dedicated, and I cannot think how the loss to Earth could be greater. During the course of this year, Sheppard had to deal with the loss of his commanding officer, the death of his father, and the abduction of a valued team-mate, and yet through all of this he continued to do his duty with admirable calm and grace. Should we prove unable to locate and rescue Colonel Sheppard and his team, it is my strongest recommendation that he be awarded a posthumous medal of honor for his outstanding service to this mission and the Air Force as a whole.

— **Colonel Samantha Carter**

COLONEL SAMANTHA CARTER

"I've come here fully committed to this expedition, to Atlantis, and most importantly, to each and every one of you."

The character of Samantha Carter really needs no introduction. Having appeared in 211 episodes over ten seasons of *Stargate SG-1*, Carter is a huge presence in the *Stargate* universe. So, when it became apparent that Atlantis would need a new commander, she seemed like the clear favorite to take over — at least from the producers' standpoint. Actress Amanda Tapping confesses that she herself required a little convincing before agreeing to take a trip to the Pegasus Galaxy.

"Joe Mallozzi and Paul Mullie contacted me and asked me if I would be at all interested in taking over as the commander of the Atlantis base," she explains. "They'd always had hopes of moving one of the *SG-1* characters over, and I think Carter was the obvious choice for them. I was very reluctant at first, to be quite honest. I thought, 'They've got such a solid cast, and I don't want to step on anyone's toes...' I had a lot of reservations. But Joe and Paul presented it in such a nice way, they had a very compelling argument and they made it sound really interesting. I was going to be in town shooting the *SG-1* movies, and I really enjoy the cast of *Atlantis* and I like the show. The way that Joe and Paul presented it, it was kind of a no-brainer. I spoke to David Hewlett about it and I spoke to Torri Higginson, because that was obviously the hardest part. And she was great. Everyone was great — Rachel was lovely, Joe was lovely. So when I agreed, I felt really good about the decision."

When integrating Carter into the Atlantis team, it was important for Tapping that she fit properly into the show's established dynamic. As a long-running lead on another series, the character is a particularly strong one, and the actress did not want Carter's shadow to loom so large in the corridors of Atlantis.

"I tried to do a different version of Carter, because I didn't want her to come in all strong-arm, bully-bully. It was partly Amanda and partly Carter, but I didn't think Carter would go in there with this ball-busting action. I thought she would go in aware that a good leader is only as good as the people that they surround themselves with, and that it was in the best interests of the project for her to play to the strengths of her people. So it was a gentler version of Carter, less acerbic in terms of her relationship with Rodney. Some of that I wish we had gotten back," Tapping adds candidly. "There was a place part way through the season where Carter felt comfortable enough in her own shoes to start the banter up again, and I wish we had, because that's something that David and I always had so much fun playing."

This altered version of Carter extended to her practical role in the show, which no longer required her to be as active — either physically or mentally — as she had been

COLONEL SAMANTHA CARTER

in *Stargate SG-1*. Finding a balance between Carter and McKay was of paramount importance. Being equals in their chosen field of science meant one of them had to step back from the problem-solving aspects of the challenges in Atlantis.

"I think at that point you couldn't bring in another McKay," says the actress. "David is so good at that and McKay is such a great character that to bring in another scientist is silly. So what they did was they made Carter the non-scientist. She was the leader and she had to defer to Rodney, because she doesn't know the Pegasus Galaxy. She doesn't know the threats or the complications."

Tapping admits that this new version of Carter was very odd to play. "The weirdest thing for me on Atlantis was not going though the gate, and being the one that they come and *talk* to about the mission. It felt so un-Carter-like, to not be pro-active," she laughs, "to get the information secondhand. I'm so used to ten years of playing a character that came in and reported to her superiors about what had happened, and who came back with the team after a mission, that camaraderie of what we've just been through. It felt very much like being an outsider. It was weird."

Carter wasn't entirely base-bound, however, and throughout the season she had plenty to do. One particularly memorable outing was in the episode 'Trio', which found Carter, Keller and McKay trapped in a hole off-world. The action of the episode mostly took place in mid-air, on a series of rafters suspended above a gimbled set. For Tapping, this was a terrifying personal challenge.

"I'm petrified of heights," she reveals. "It's one of my biggest phobias. So what was interesting was my character is the only one that's supposed to be really comfortable up there, and I was *scared*. We had a great rigging team, but when we first went into rehearsal and climbed these ladders over to these rafters — I was petrified. There was one time in particular where I had to walk across the beam and then turn around. And I couldn't do it. I froze, and I panicked. I remember looking at David and Jewel and saying, 'I'm petrified right now. I literally can't move.' The rigging guy crawled across the rafter and grabbed my hand and pulled me back. It was really scary — and embarrassing, because I'm pretty proud! But there I am up on this rafter, in tears, and I can't get down.

"I ended up overcoming it to a degree and getting quite comfortable after a while," Tapping adds. "By the end of the shoot I was like a completely different person. Doing some of the crawling up the boxes to the very top of the set, I quite enjoyed that. When I had boxes in front of me, when I had something to climb, I was actually quite comfortable. Standing up on those rafters with nothing to hold on to was really scary."

As it turned out, Carter's tour of duty in the Pegasus Galaxy would be a relatively short one. Following the end of shooting on season four, Tapping realized that she was finally going to have to let go of playing Samantha Carter in a regular capacity.

PROGRESS REPORT
Colonel Samantha Carter

I hardly feel qualified to assess my first year as leader of Atlantis in my own words. The assignment was, while not wholly expected, a welcome one. I had of course read of the many challenges facing the expedition, and although I arrived in the wake of tragic circumstances, I feel privileged to have served as part of the Pegasus expedition. The men and women of Atlantis are an extraordinary group of people — amazingly talented, and all willing to sacrifice themselves to explore the Pegasus Galaxy and learn about its cultures. Above all, I feel honored to have been accepted so readily by these people, and although it has not been an easy year, I am pleased to have stood beside them as they experienced it. I know that Richard Woolsey did not always approve of my methods — but a situation such as this requires flexibility. If my years on SG-1 taught me to stand in the face of adversity, then my first twelve months in the Pegasus Galaxy have shown me what it is to wait while others carry out the command to do the same.

— **Colonel Samantha Carter**

Sanctuary, the show created by former *Stargate SG-1* producer Damian Kindler and produced by Kindler, Tapping and Martin Wood, was waiting for word of being picked up for a thirteen-episode run. As it teetered on a knife-edge, the actress realized that she had to make a choice.

"At first I was like, 'We can make this work, we can make this work… I can do ten episodes [of *Atlantis*], I can do five of them now, we can…' But it was just going to be impossible timing-wise. Joe and Paul said, 'We can't have you as the first lead on another series and hope to get you whenever we can. It's just not fair.' And I totally got that. It *wasn't* fair — and it wasn't fair for me to turn my back on all these people who had been holding out for *Sanctuary*. I couldn't turn my back on them. In the end I had to take a leap of faith that *Sanctuary* would go. It was a tremendous leap. I was bawling my eyes out in my last conversation with Joe Mallozzi. He was like, 'What's wrong?' And I said, 'Eleven years! Eleven years with this character, and I'm done. It's over.'" Å

DR RODNEY MCKAY

"Asking me to do performance evaluations is ridiculous. I am the first to admit I don't know who these people are, nor do I care to."

Now, we all know that McKay is used to being the smartest person on the Atlantis expedition. At least, that's what he delights in telling us. Regularly. But season four brought in a character that could well challenge that assertion — and indeed, she had been for years, ever since they first butted heads in the laboratories of Stargate Command.

Bringing Colonel Carter to Atlantis was a curious challenge for actor David Hewlett. After all, Carter's role in SG-1 was essentially what McKay's role is in Atlantis. They're the smart ones, the ones that understand the science bit, the ones that can drag the team out of trouble and save the galaxy with math, bits of wire and an idea. Striking a balance that didn't challenge the two characters traditional roles was key.

"It was interesting," Hewlett recalls, "because we talked about that a bunch of times. 'You step on my toes, you're going down,' is basically what I said to her, and she was obviously scared and intimidated. She backed *right* off!" he jokes. "No, we talked about it a number of times. I remember the first episode I ever did, on *SG-1*, she would go through some of her reactions to stuff that I wanted to do, and then I would push stuff further because she was being so open. On the day it's just magic to have an actor who's as open as that, especially a lead on a show, because you just get so wrapped up in, 'Oh my god, what scene is next?' that it's not always easy to sit down with the person that you don't work with all the time and do that. We did the same with this. We came in, and there were lines where we were saying things like, 'I know this is what she should say but the reality is, this is how she *feels*, so we're going to square off on this'. We built arguments into things that weren't said. It adds a really nice energy to the scene, because there's so much going on the whole time.

"The other thing about Carter is that she's good at delegating. Yes she can fly in and save the day and that's what she did on *SG-1*, and to some extent that's what I do on *Atlantis*, but the reality was she was in charge and she had to delegate. And that's what Amanda said to me: 'Well, I may know a lot about SG-1, but you know a lot about Atlantis. So what I know, I know, and what you know, you know. And together we can pool this stuff.' So it was great. And naturally," he adds, deadpan, "she's terrified of me…"

As it happened, McKay had quite a lot to take his mind off Carter throughout his latest year on Atlantis. He broke up with his girlfriend, was reunited with his dead best buddy, fell in love, and changed the course of Earth history with a plan ten thousand years in the execution. It's enough to keep anyone rather busy.

DR RODNEY MCKAY

The first of those monumental incidents was the unexpected resolution of McKay's slow-burning romance with botanist Dr Katie Brown, played by Brenda James. The relationship had got off to a rather unconventional start in season two, during 'Duet', in which McKay had to share his consciousness with Lieutenant Cadman. 'Quarantine' saw McKay — in his usual clumsy and rather ill-advised way — actively trying to move it forward by means of a marriage proposal.

"That was fantastic. I just loved it because it was so frustrating. It's like, so McKay's got the beautiful and lovely Katie Brown locked in basically a tropical paradise. He's got a ring. The man is set! And he screws it up. How do you screw that up? Now admittedly, it was a tiny diamond, but I don't think she would have cared… But it was funny. I think this is a great episode because he panics all the time about stuff, and 'Quarantine' is a great example of him panicking about the wrong stuff. It's nice to see that yes, he can panic and solve the problem most of the time, but there are days when that's not going to happen. And this is one of those times. He has no computer and he's screwed. There's nothing he can do, it's not in his realm of expertise."

Hewlett agrees with the script's notion that it was time to have some sort of culmination to the couple's story, though he reveals that at the time, he had a slightly different attitude to that final goodbye scene. "It was definitely one of those ones that I originally thought I would leave more open," he recalls. "And then I think Martin Wood was very eager to push that into McKay realizing what's going on. It's written pretty open-ended. It really allowed a lot for the performance there. It's saying goodbye without realizing you've said goodbye until afterwards. There's a lot of history with her and it did need to move on. My big joke is that she's probably going to be dating Zelenka next. It'd just drive McKay crazy. Also I'd just really like her to come back! Brenda is just absolutely lovely, and is again one of those actresses with absolutely no attitude, so it was just nice having her around."

The season culminated with far-reaching episode 'The Last Man', which projects a future for McKay that is far from settled and includes much tragedy for the character.

"I read it and I was a bit worried about it, to be honest with you," Hewlett confesses. "There was so much talking! There's always that fear. I don't want to be the guy that, when people tune into the show, they go, 'Oh, it's that guy talking again.' So I actually went upstairs [to the producers] and I questioned a lot of it. But the reality is that when I saw it, I really liked that episode. It really came together. You forget, because when you shoot, you shoot all the talking! You're in for three days and you shoot three days of *talking*. So you feel like you become very McKay-centric, and you think the show is just about you because that's all you see. But then when you sit down and watch the show — I was moved by it, it's really quite plaintive and sad. It's the complete destruction of this whole little family because of a couple of mistakes. So I was quite touched by it."

PROGRESS REPORT
Dr Rodney McKay

It is no secret that Dr McKay and I have shared a long working relationship. It was, I admit, with some trepidation that I approached my new situation as his superior. Not, I hasten to add, because I was concerned about his reaction, but rather because I felt my presence may cause him professional concern. We are, after all, both leaders in our field of science. I decided to make a clear delineation between my skills as a scientist and my position as leader of Atlantis, and this seemed to work. The past year has turned up many challenges that required his expertise, and he has once again risen to the tasks presented to him. He also seems to have mellowed somewhat over the years, and though his arrogance is still as much a part of him as ever, he has made efforts to integrate more with his colleagues. The ordeal that he shared with his sister, Jeannie Miller, had the most profound effect on him — more than I think he will admit. Towards the end of the year, I have to confess that I think we were actually becoming friends... though perhaps that is saying too much.

— **Colonel Samantha Carter**

'The Last Man' coincided with another momentous event, this time in the actor's personal life, as his first child was due in the same week that the episode was shot.

"We were waiting for him to be born, and I kept saying to them, 'Guys... I'm in four hours of prosthetics, and you know that the moment I get that phone call, these four hours of prosthetics and this actor will be leaving. You're going to be screwed!'" The actor's solution was to give some of the talking to another character. Hewlett laughs, remembering. "I tried everything. I was like, 'Wouldn't *Carter* say this? This seems like something Carter would say...' But it actually worked out beautifully, and he was born literally the next day. He's a producer's son! His timing was impeccable." Å

TELYA EMMAGAN

"You were right to question my involvement in this mission. There was a time I would have laid down my life for you, or Ronon, or Rodney, without hesitation. But, I have other considerations now."

The fourth year of *Stargate: Atlantis* was a tumultuous one, not only for Teyla, but also for actress Rachel Luttrell. Discovering the happy news that she was expecting her first child early on in the season, Luttrell's first worry was how to break the news to the show's producers. Bridge Studios is no stranger to new motherhood — both Amanda Tapping and Claudia Black (Vala Mal Doran) had experienced pregnancy whilst working on *Stargate SG-1*. Luttrell's baby, however, would be a first for *Stargate: Atlantis*.

"Oh god — was I nervous? Petrified. I was absolutely *petrified*," the actress laughs. "The very first call that I made was to Amanda Tapping, before I called the producers. I called Amanda first, and left her this coy little message that I thought was hiding the fact. But she got it right away! She called me back and said, 'Oh my goodness…' We had this lovely little conversation. I wanted to talk to her because it's something that she dealt with herself, with her little one. She's such a lovely person, and she said, 'Well, you know what, I'm going to be there on Monday for a wardrobe fitting, so why don't you come by then? Swing by the wardrobe department and we'll have a little chitchat and I'll hold your hand. And if you want me to come up there with you I will.' So I called the producers and said, 'There's something I'd like to talk to you about…' I showed up on that Monday and sure enough, there was Amanda. We had our little talk and then I went up and dropped the bomb, as it were. Yeah, I was very nervous. I didn't know how they were going to take it."

A pregnant actress will always present issues that the producers need to resolve, however open and sympathetic to the notion they may be. Even if they decide to write the pregnancy into the story, as the writers of *Stargate: Atlantis* did, it's sure to mean large changes not only for the character, but those around her. If the birth is expected during filming, there's the question of how to cover the actress's absence, not to mention wardrobe issues, and so on. With Teyla, it was further complicated by the fact that she's a particularly active character. If there's hand-to-hand combat, Teyla's likely to be involved somewhere, and for season four, new show runners Joseph Mallozzi and Paul Mullie had been planning to push that even further.

"They had been talking to me about how season four was going to be very Teyla-dominant," Luttrell explains, "and I knew that [my pregnancy] was going to require them to shift gears quite a bit. But you know, they took it in their stride and ran with it, and I think we got quite a few wonderful storylines out of it, not just for me but for

the other characters. It allowed us as actors to get a lot more emotional, and for the characters to reveal how they really feel about each other and how far they would go for each other. That all came about with me dropping the bomb!"

One of the most powerful scenes in the story of Teyla's pregnancy is when she finally reveals her condition to John Sheppard. Conducted in one of Atlantis's functional hallways, at a point not of her choosing, it's an uncomfortable and emotional moment between the two.

"That's what I mean about my pregnancy bringing about all kinds of deepening emotions for the characters," Luttrell points out, "in terms of how they feel about each other. Joe and I talked about that scene and how we wanted to play it. We read it a few times together and worked on the beats. Joe decided that for him, there was a certain amount of jealousy, because obviously there's *something* between the characters, and he wanted to play that. We both wanted to play the fact that they are quite close. This is a huge thing that she was keeping from him and he was a little hurt about that as well. There are so many levels between the two of them. I think their characters have always had a bond, and I hope that it came across."

As it happened, Rachel's pregnancy contributed to season four being one of the most Teyla-heavy seasons of *Stargate: Atlantis* to date. The actress has long desired to investigate more about her character's connection to her people and the Wraith. 'Missing' kicked off a storyline that would do just that, weaving together Teyla's pregnancy and her search for her people.

"I remember doing some of the biggest fight scenes that I had done to date, all the while knowing that I was three months pregnant! Yeah," she laughs wryly, "that was a huge episode on so many levels. Half of our crew knew about me being pregnant and half of them didn't, and I dropped the bomb to a couple of other people as we were filming."

One of the most important people to know was stunt coordinator James 'BamBam' Bamford. Besides being a close friend, BamBam had to know simply so he could choreograph Teyla's fights accordingly and book in doubles as and when they were needed.

"We told all the stunt performers and I had told BamBam weeks before. I got to fight my husband in one of the fight sequences — he was a Bola Kai, one of the warriors! But I ended up doing quite sizeable chunks of all those fight sequences. The only things that they stopped

PROGRESS REPORT
Teyla Emmagan

As a woman in Earth's military, I understand what it is to train and go into battle side by side with men. Even in these enlightened days, it is not easy. Within short hours of meeting Teyla Emmagan, I realized that her ability as a fighter and her courage under fire, coupled with her depth of humanity gave me reason to respect her even more than I already did from Dr Weir's previous reports. Teyla's compassion and empathy — qualities often used to discriminate against women in Earth's military — make her a stronger, more capable warrior. I feel that the IOA would do well to look at her as an example of what women can achieve if they are treated as true equals to their male counterparts. Even in pregnancy, Teyla proved herself a valuable part of my team. Without her, Atlantis is a lesser place, and I will do all in my power to find her — and her child.

— **Colonel Samantha Carter**

me doing, and things that I wouldn't have done anyway, were places where I had to hit the ground hard."

The conditions of the location shoot were harsh — it was early in the year in Vancouver, B.C., and the more clement weather of spring and summer had yet to arrive. "I remember being out in the cold and the rain," Luttrell says, "and working with Jewel. The two of us were just so freezing cold. Jewel and I car-pooled together to get to the location, and she was my saving grace. We had a lot of laughs in moments where things could have been miserable. And this bridge that they made for us — good *god*! I remember seeing that for the first time and saying, 'You've *got* to be kidding me! I am *not* walking out on that!'" she laughs. "That was amazing. But we had a lot of fun." Å

RONON DEX

"When you find someone to point a gun at, you let me know."

*S*targate: *Atlantis*'s fourth year proved momentous for Ronon Dex, who found himself once again questioning his place in the city. Having said a touching goodbye to Weir in 'Adrift', in which he thanked her for giving him a place to live when he had nowhere else to go, Ronon suddenly discovered that he was not the only survivor of his home planet after all. 'Reunion' gave actor Jason Momoa a real chance to stretch his acting muscles, and saw Ronon the warrior considering leaving the friends he had made for the friends he had rediscovered.

"I think it was great for my character," says Momoa of the episode. "To know that my best friend is alive was pretty amazing. It was just cool for Ronon to let his guard down and have hope for the future — that he can go on missions, be his own boss and do his own thing with the Atlanteans, but also with his family, his Satedan friends."

Of course, nothing is ever quite what it seems in the Pegasus Galaxy. Ronon's betrayal at the hands of his long-lost friends was complete and tragic — but as far as the actor is concerned, it provided the catalyst for Dex to realize where he really belonged. "It was interesting for me," he says. "When he was betrayed, he found out that Atlantis *is* his home."

The episode also provided an added practical bonus for Momoa, which, as he explains, had to do with the way in which the production cast the role of Tyre.

"On a stunt level — sometimes we get actors that are actors and not stunt people, and then we have to hire someone else to do the stunts. But I did all my stunts with Mark Dacascos, who is a great stunt guy."

Stunts have always been a key element of playing the Satedan — Ronon's fighting abilities are central to the character's popularity. In season four, those fights went up a notch or two. It's something that the actor completely approves of, because it's that aspect of the character that he most enjoys.

"They've been going up every year," Momoa says with enthusiasm. "If we've already done it, we try not to duplicate it. BamBam and I have come up with a style for Ronon and we try to keep inside the context of what I can do in that style of fighting. For example, he's not a kicker — he's a head-butter, a puncher. And BamBam's got great ideas. He's a fabulous artist and comes up with great fights and it just gets better and better. You get two guys together doing what they love, it's always going to be good."

Another curveball for Ronon in season four is the unexpected frisson that develops between him and Jennifer Keller during the events of 'Quarantine'. Though Momoa doesn't think those moments necessarily meant anything for the character in the long

term — and points out that he's been alone for a long time. "That was only really one episode," he says. "It's weird, because I don't see Ronon settling down with anyone. His true love is lost. And who knows — maybe they had kids that are still out there. You can go anywhere with it. I just don't see him settling down — he's still an outsider and he's got to have that edge. It would be like Samson losing his hair!"

Of course, the big thing for Ronon in season four was something that the fans had been waiting for since *Stargate: Atlantis* first came to the screen. And in 'Midway', it finally happened. Ronon Dex and Teal'c came face to face — and then some!

"I've heard all the myths and stories about him," laughs Momoa of guest star Christopher Judge. "He can brighten up a room like no one I've ever seen. He's an enigma, that one! I loved it, I loved how we were so evenly matched. Chris Judge didn't need a stunt guy at all, he did everything himself and he was amazing. I've got so much respect for that guy. It was a great episode, directed by Andy Mikita, whom I love. He was jazzed because he's a huge Judge fan. He did a great job on that script."

Having the two characters come together for the episode really gave Momoa and Judge a chance to push them to the very limit. Of course, fans wanted to see them fight side by side eventually — but it was clear that there was going to be friction to begin with, especially since Teal'c was there at Carter's behest, to 'train' Ronon before his meeting with the IOA. Momoa felt it was important for Ronon to make his feelings clear — and found the perfect chance to do so with the cafeteria scene in which Teal'c skillfully makes his point by insulting Sateda's defeat by the Wraith.

"That was fantastic," Momoa grins. "I get pissed at him! I actually threw the table in the first take we did. I didn't tell Judge that's what I was going to do, I just grabbed the table and went, 'Raarrrgh!' and lifted it up. He didn't even break face."

The move hadn't been rehearsed, and though Judge wasn't fazed by the unscripted action, the crew was rather taken by surprise!

"I didn't want to tell them," Momoa explains, "because if you tell them, they'd be like, 'No, bad idea.' But I said, 'You don't have to use it. You can take it out. But he's talking crap about my people and *this* is how Ronon would react.' So we did that and they didn't use it, but I did push the food off the table. It was a fun scene. I did it really angry first off, and then I did a take where I just internalized it, like putting a lid on the pot and it all bubbled up. It worked really well. Joe [Flanigan] came up and said, 'That was good,' which was nice. It's always nice to have a co-star like what you do." Å

PROGRESS REPORT
Ronon Dex

Ronon, while a very capable warrior, is still very young and prone to the sort of impetuousness that I thought I had left behind when General O'Neill was promoted away from active duty. Our first meeting did not go well — and I suspect that after the incident with his Satedan friends he thought I was going to be difficult to work with. When Ronon comes up against an obstacle, his first instinct is to blast his way through it, and that approach did not sit well with me. Colonel Sheppard continually assured me that Ronon was simply "rough around the edges", but although I trusted Sheppard and was impressed with the clear bond between them, I was still not sure of Ronon. My decision to ask Teal'c to help coach him grew out of this concern, and though at first I feared I had been wrong, I think their work together really signaled the beginning of a new chapter for Ronon. He is a valued, and valuable, member of the Atlantis team, and I am glad that the IOA chose to recognize his contribution to the Pegasus expedition.

— **Colonel Samantha Carter**

DR JENNIFER KELLER

"I signed up to be chief of medicine on an expedition in a whole other galaxy. That's about as challenging as it gets. But eating gross food, sorry, but that's where I draw the line."

Though Dr Keller had appeared briefly at the conclusion of season three, viewers didn't really have a chance to get to know her until season four. In actual fact, had circumstances been different, audiences may have seen her much sooner and in a very different role. Jewel Staite had previously appeared in season two, as the Wraith child Ellia in 'Instinct', and the producers liked her performance so much that they immediately thought about extending Ellia's life.

"After I did the episode in season two they asked if I was interested in coming back to play the Wraith again," Staite explains. "I said, 'Well, I love the show and I love the people that I'm working with, but I don't want to go through that make-up every day!' So luckily about a year later they called and said, 'How about playing a doctor?' And that was that — I was signed on!"

The character of Keller enjoys a very slow burn throughout season four, and it takes a long time for her to start revealing bits and pieces about her life and personality. The actress reports that she had the same experience, in that when she agreed to take the part, Keller was still something of a mystery. "I kind of had to play the guessing game a little bit," she laughs. "They said that she was very smart, calm, cool and collected in the operating room, that was her element. But once she was *out* of her element she was very sensitive to the world of violence and guns and that kind of thing, and was nervous and didn't necessarily believe in her abilities. That was something very different for me to play, but that's what makes it so much fun. She's got all these different sides to her personality."

One of the earliest chances viewers had to see Keller "out of her element" was during the events of 'Missing'. After taking a trip with Teyla to visit her people, the two women find themselves stranded and pursued — and Keller definitely has to push herself beyond her usual boundaries.

"I loved that one, that one was really fun," Staite exclaims. "The best part was that it was me and Rachel. We get on really well, and we have a whole load of inside jokes and stupid things that we do to make each other laugh and make the hours pass by."

'Missing' was also a chance for the production team to see just how far Staite would go in the pursuit of her craft — and she impressed them all by being pretty much game for anything. One of the most spectacular scenes in the episode involves a rope bridge, which had been built by the production but was still a rather daunting prospect to cross. It was high, it was narrow, and it was in the middle of nowhere.

"I never get chosen to do action," she laughs. "I'm always the person on the sidelines, cheering people on. So I'm always really excited when they give me things to do where I'm not just scared and hiding in a corner and I get to be a little bit of a hero. I was really excited at the end, when Dr Keller steps up to the plate and saves the day. It was cool, and it's always fun learning stunts and fight sequences. You feel like such a bad ass! The bridge wasn't too bad. At the beginning of the day it looked really scary, but once I walked across it once, it was fine. I was in a harness and I was hooked up to the bridge and there were all these safety guys. I felt quite safe. Shooting outside is always really difficult — it was rainy and cold, and so that episode seemed to drag on and on. But often the episodes that are the most difficult to film are the best. I was so happy that it turned out well."

Later in the season, 'Quarantine' revealed a little more about Keller's background, painting the picture of a lonely adolescence. "I was relieved," the actress confesses of learning the character's backstory, "because I had assumed that she didn't have much of a social life when she was growing up and she was pressured into succeeding and doing well and was probably immersed in academics and that kind of thing. I was really happy that I had assumed right! And I loved that she was vulnerable enough with Ronon to admit that. I really liked that."

Another Keller-heavy episode that further solidified the character and her relationships with her fellow Atlantis team-mates was 'Trio'. For Staite, filming the episode was not only a chance to explore Keller's relationships with Carter and McKay, but also a considerable challenge to perform.

"I was really happy to know that it was going to be David and Amanda with me in the hole. We knew that it was going to be dirty and dusty in there and once they have the wind machines going in a dusty set on one of these sound stages, it's hard to breathe and it's kind of gross. But Amanda and David are hilarious — the three of us are probably the 'bad kids' on the set, we tell the most jokes, we ruin the most takes. So it was really good because there was no pressure to behave," the actress laughs, "because I knew that probably one of them was going to get into more trouble than I was! We had such a blast. That was by far my favorite to film. We laughed the entire time, and just had such a great time. Despite it being difficult, it was actually really fun."

The steep learning curve around Keller culminated in the season finale, 'Last Man', which sped her life forward through several unexpected turns of events and into a tragically early death.

"I was a little surprised by that one," Staite admits, "just because I wasn't sure how they were going to handle the McKay-Keller relationship. We sort of went into that a little bit at the end of 'Trio', which I really liked. I think they're an interesting match, they have a lot of similarities that they probably don't even know about. So I was surprised but I was also really excited about it. I loved that Keller was able to step up to the plate with Woolsey. She defends her position and has that inner strength to take a stand and leave. She decides that she's not going to support what he's doing. And then

PROGRESS REPORT
Dr Jennifer Keller

I had seen several IOA comments, prior to meeting Dr Keller myself, that made mention of her youth and presented concerns about her abilities to perform as Atlantis's chief medical officer. Having now served with Keller for a year, I can safely guarantee that such concerns are completely unwarranted. Dr Keller, besides being an expert in her field, has shown an exemplary ability to adapt to situations that I feel many older, more experienced medical professionals would shy from. Her calm, pleasant manner has provided a wonderful additional dynamic to the command team. Her courage in the face of adversity is to be commended, and I myself have witnessed first hand her ability to deal with unimaginable pressure effectively. I can honestly say that, bar Dr Beckett, Atlantis could have no better chief of medicine.

— **Colonel Samantha Carter**

of course the death scene with McKay is quite sad. I really liked how she went out with a bit of dignity and said that she had no regrets — I thought that was quite sweet."

Dr Keller made herself such an invaluable part of the *Atlantis* line-up so quickly that it wasn't long before the show's producers were considering making her a more permanent addition to the series. Within one season, Keller went from a recurring character to a regular, an arrangement Staite was more than happy with.

"They called in the fall and told me that we had been picked up for a fifth season," she explains. "Once contract negotiations began, they asked if I was willing to come on for more time, and I was more than happy to join. It's a great show, a great cast. It's a very easy set to be on, but at the same time, there are all these extreme situations that we're playing out every week, so it's fun. You never really know what your character is going to go through next, so it's a bit of a challenge as well, which is good." Å

"Save it. You're not going anywhere 'til I get some answers. I need to know what you've done to my people." — *Lorne*

S eason four had a large complement of familiar faces returning to various roles throughout the year. *Stargate: Atlantis* had always held up the tantalizing possibility of crossovers with *Stargate SG-1*. With the arrival of Carter and the real-life conclusion of *SG-1*'s long run came the chance to see another much-loved character grace the halls of Atlantis: namely Teal'c, played by **Christopher Judge**. Fans had long debated who would come out on top in a showdown between the former Jaffa warrior and Ronon Dex. The question wasn't actually answered in 'Midway' — after all, who really wants to see either of these great characters defeated at the hand of the other? Instead, the pair proved just what a fantastic team they make!

Below: Christopher Judge as Teal'c.

Another former *Stargate SG-1* character that resurfaced in season four was Dr Bill Lee, played by science fiction stalwart **Bill Dow**. The hapless doctor had previously appeared in season two's 'Critical Mass' and season three's two-parter, 'The Return'. For season four, however, he finally made it out of Stargate Command, tagging along in 'Adrift' as Colonel Carter tried to locate Atlantis.

"I was happy," laughs Dow of seeing that in the script, "because it never makes it into the shows, but whenever we're sitting in my lab and discover that there's some kind of horrible problem that needs to be dealt with off-world, and they all start packing up and start heading out the door in their usual heroic fashion, after the dialogue of the scene is over, I always go, 'Can I come? Can I come?' And they all go, 'No!' So in the outtakes there are always tons of that. So I

was quite happy to be out there!"

Kavan Smith, who returned in season four, has a surprisingly long history as Major Evan Lorne. The character first appeared way back in *Stargate SG-1*'s seventh season as a geologist attached to Stargate Command in the episode 'Enemy Mine'. In fact, Smith had gone up for the part of Daniel Jackson six years earlier. Later on, when the actor auditioned for the part in *Stargate: Atlantis* that would eventually become Lorne, it was originally conceived as an entirely different character. But director Martin Wood, having decided that Smith was the man for the part, suggested that the character become Lorne. And his move to the Pegasus Galaxy was complete.

"It started as such a minor character," says Smith, "even though they used him a fair bit. For the first season or two he was really just whatever I decided he was going to be. And then, as they used him more, they started adding little things. The painting thing came out of nowhere," he laughs. "I hadn't put that anywhere in my character breakdown! But they're adding more and more, and they've given me a pretty decent sense of humor, I think, especially when I get to work with either of the Davids [Hewlett and Nykl]. They like to clash Zelenka and I together, and Lorne definitely has a bit of a love-hate relationship with Rodney!"

Katie Brown, played by **Brenda James**, has been a part of *Stargate: Atlantis* since season two, when she caught the eye of Rodney McKay in the episode 'Duet'. The

Above left: Bill Dow as Dr Bill Lee, with David Hewlett as Dr Rodney McKay.
Above: Kavan Smith as Major Evan Lorne.

character had two significant episodes in the show's fourth year, the second of which may well prove to be the last time we see her.

"I was really excited," says James of the episode 'Quarantine'. "I kept hoping that Rodney and Katie would get together and have a romantic moment. I think that was Katie," she adds, laughing. "I think Katie was really hoping that here they are, they've got some time together, maybe they would become a little closer."

In the event, things really didn't happen that way, and the episode's ending becomes rather a sad moment.

Below: Brenda James as Katie Brown.

James reveals that writer Carl Binder actually came to set for that part of filming, anxious that the scene came together as he had envisioned it.

"I think when I came into it originally, I was actually harder," she says. "I think I came into it thinking that by the end I was more turned off by McKay. But the director and the writer really wanted to make sure that there was still some warmth between us, and when they told me that, I really enjoyed the ending much more. I think that's more appropriate to Katie's character, because I think that's who she is. She's not a hard person, and I think she really does care for McKay. It was more about the sadness and the possibility of loss than about me not liking him. And I think it was more poignant with their direction."

Robert Picardo has now played IOA bureaucrat Richard Woolsey for five years. This season, sent to appraise Colonel Carter in her new position as commander of Atlantis, he found himself once again

confronted by the harsh realities of life in the field. For Picardo, the chance to take Woolsey to Atlantis was one he was very happy to explore — despite the character's experiences at the hands of the Asurans in season three.

"I've enjoyed not only playing the character but also the experience of working with both casts," says the science fiction veteran, who is famous for his role as the holographic Doctor on *Star Trek: Voyager.* "The writer/producers have treated me very nicely and I think rather amazingly rehabilitated a character who was originally introduced, not so much as a villain, but as an unpleasant bureaucrat. He was sent in to assign blame after the tragic death of Dr Fraiser [in the *SG-1* episode 'Heroes']. Woolsey comes in as a bulldog so that someone's head will roll appropriately. But for my next appearance, they rehabilitated him quite a bit. They made him a guy that may rub people the wrong way and may be annoying, but at least he means well. He has a high ethical standard and thinks that military operations need to have civilian oversight to stop them spinning out of control. He's shown a certain courage and backbone."

Above: Robert Picardo as Richard Woolsey.

Season four also featured the return, with a vengeance, of Atlantis's arch-enemy, Michael. Played by **Connor Trinneer**, the character has proved a significant thorn in the team's side since season two. This year, however, we might just be persuaded to forgive him, since, though his latest plan involved kidnapping Teyla and threatening her baby, it also provided for the miraculous return of **Paul McGillion** as Dr Carson Beckett. It just goes to show that there's a bit of good in everyone — even if it's inadvertent! Å

VALERIE HALVERSON

For costume designer Val Halverson, *Stargate: Atlantis*'s fourth year presented an opportunity to do something a little different for the production. Actually, season four meant a lot of changes for the costume department, some expected and some unexpected — but then, the ever-cheerful Halverson and her staff are always up for a challenge. Which is just as well, given their workload and the timescales to which they operate.

"I was coming on as a new designer," Halverson explains, from her colorfully cluttered office at Bridge Studios, "so it was an opportunity, and they felt that there were some changes that needed to be made. With Amanda Tapping coming on to the team we were able to freshen it up a bit, and address some of the concerns that the producers had about the look of the team. We wanted to give them a few more layers in their look, because they were basically in their uniforms most of the time. I did some homework on the last three seasons and really felt that we could individualize them more."

Halverson went to work designing a new off-world look to the team's costumes, which still incorporated enough of the original style that they fitted with the rest of the Atlantis background. After all, the city is a busy place, and there was no way that the costume department could afford — or would even have time — to change the uniform of every visible member of the Atlantis expedition. Instead they worked on the lead team's look, giving them sleeker outfits with details that spoke to each character's individual personality — for example, a close inspection of McKay's intricate jacket reveals a section of circuitboard to denote his 'resident science genius' status.

Below: Halverson created beautiful maternity wear for Teyla.

"They all got this sexy look, definitive to their character. McKay's got a circuitboard. And Carter was new this year — she got a really sexy outfit and she looked dynamite. It was a work of love because we love Amanda — and she's been in military gear for ten years so she was very excited about it too!"

Of course, year four also meant designing costumes for Rachel

Luttrell, whose pregnancy would play out throughout the course of the season. In some ways, Teyla's alien roots were a blessing for the costume department, since the audience was already accustomed to seeing the character in outfits other than the standard Pegasus expedition uniforms. Altering such an outfit to accommodate a pregnancy would have been a lot more problematic, but Teyla's Athosian wardrobe gave Halverson a little leeway.

"Rachel did have to let us know pretty early on and we did see changes pretty quickly, but they were fairly small to start with," recalls the designer. "Of course, we had to have a discussion with our producers and directors about how they wanted to proceed with that. Often they will try to hide it right through to the end, which is very difficult to do from a costume point of view. Luckily, our writers and producers were excited about using it in the storyline, but we couldn't release that information for quite a long time so we did have to hide it with the use of computer screens and all sorts of other things. It was very interesting to try to find a way to make her look as sexy as always as she was getting more voluptuous, while still hiding her tummy. Teyla always had a bare stomach as part of her costume and we made that a gradual change so that the fans wouldn't necessarily pick up on it right away. We tried to keep her very Athosian. Teyla often wore a uniform with an Athosian top under that, so we kept that feel and her uniforms just changed a little bit. But so often in TV it's a shot from the waist up rather than a full-length, so that helped us a bit as well."

COSTUMES

Halverson's job was further complicated by the fact that so much of season four had to be shot out of order to accommodate various scheduling issues. So episodes shot first, when Luttrell's pregnancy was barely visible, would be shown much later in the season, while episodes shot late on, when her pregnancy was more obvious, would be shown earlier. As the season went on, and Teyla revealed her pregnancy to her colleagues, the challenge of hiding her stomach lessened. For the costume department, however, the challenge had just begun!

"We actually had one episode, 'The Kindred', where we had five outfits for her and we had to almost fit them daily. The episode went for two weeks, so what fit her at the beginning of the episode didn't fit her halfway through, because at that point she really was changing daily. It was a huge challenge! Just having the difference, the variety of sizes, is a challenge," Halverson says, "and it's a challenge to see what works best on each person. But if they're all the same size then you can get into a bit of a rut, so I always enjoy that."

In the event, Teyla's outfits in year four are some of her most beautiful to date, and that's a trend that continued throughout the season on different episodes. For the episode 'Spoils of War', the audience was introduced to the idea of Wraith reproduction and a new Queen with one of the most striking costumes ever conceived of for *Stargate: Atlantis*.

"That was amazing for us, because we were working with James Robbins, our production designer. We worked many weeks on that one. Thank god we got a heads-up that it was going to happen and we had the chair to work with! It was great. It took a long time to produce that costume. Initially, we were going to make the dress weave into the chair, and when she stood up it was going to look like part of the chair. We started with that research and development which we did for a couple of weeks, working with the model shop and the art department."

After consultation, a different direction was suggested, and the costume evolved further. "Our director and producers decided that they wanted her chair to grow over her costume," Halverson explains, "so that her costume needed to be a separate entity. We did that and still had to work with all the pieces of the chair that were being built by the model shop. So we made a sort of blanket that went over her and then just hooked it onto the chair. It was really a collaborative effort, and of course when all these veins and almost umbilical cords were placed over her, her costume still had to show, and so that was a unique challenge as well."

Later in the season, the episode 'Outcast' brought Sheppard and Ronon to Earth to chase down an escaped Replicator, bringing a multitude of new approaches for Halverson's team.

"Putting our cast into civilian clothes is not always as easy as one might think," she says with a laugh. "We have Jason Momoa, and our Ronon character does *not* buy anything off the rack! He has a really earthy, eclectic look to him, and we have to try

and really hold that in his character. So putting him in jeans and a T-shirt — though he would look great — is not really true to his character. So that was a challenge, but we found a few things and broke them down."

When creating Earth versions of a character's costume, the designer always makes sure to involve the actor in the design process. The costume can't be responsible for taking the actor out of his or her character's personality, so understanding what their thoughts are on how the character would dress in the present day is very important.

"Nobody knows the character better than that actor and the writers, and so we work pretty closely with them," Halverson says. "Especially when there's going to be a change like that, where they're going to go into a civilian look. I always have dialogue with all the actors about how they want to be presented."

'Outcast' also featured another unique costume in the shape of the fleeing Replicator. "He was being shot and he was steel underneath, so that was something we had to figure out with our special effects guys," the designer explains. "We made a layer underneath that was a sleek silver costume, so when we blew holes in it, it was revealed. But our model shop and our special effects guys also had plates that were put underneath, so which one was revealed depended on what kind of gun shot him. We made him eight costumes, all in different states, because of course we never shoot in sequence!"

Above: Halverson's team worked closely with the special effects department to create the costumes for 'Outcast'.

COSTUMES

The sheer volume of work that Halverson's team accomplishes for each single episode is astounding. The costume department occupies part of the lower level of the Bridge Studio production offices, beside Stage 5 (otherwise known as Stargate Command and the gateroom) and below the production offices that house the writers and producers. Their rooms are a constant blur of color and movement, with rolls of fabric piled up everywhere, and rows of costumes hanging waiting either to be worn immediately or worked on for the next day's shoot.

"Right now I have eight people working in the shop — cutters, sewers, breakdown artists, fabric workers. We have three on set and the assistant designer and myself. So it's a pretty big team full time, full tilt!"

Full tilt is certainly right. For a general episode, Halverson will have seven days to prepare all the costumes she needs for a shoot, though in special cases — for example, the Wraith chair in 'Spoils of War' — production designer James Robbins will give her a much-appreciated "heads-up". Usually, an episode will require two or three 'featured' costumes, meaning outfits not part of the usual line-up of uniforms and background performers, but that number can go up, sometimes to six or more. And each of those costumes needs multiples for shooting.

Below: Larrin (Jill Wagner) and her fellow 'travelers'.

Halverson's team lessen their workload — and their budget — as much as possible by using *Stargate*'s vast store of past costumes for the background performers who always pepper an episode. "We have an off-sight storage facility, like *Raiders of the Lost Ark*," she laughs. "It's pretty big. We've had ten years of *Stargate SG-1* and now our fifth season of *Stargate: Atlantis*. All of that has been amalgamated together to build our villages and we just keep trying to blend them together in a different way. We like to put our money into the featured costumes, and we try to do the best we can with the background."

Even when a new costume comes off the production line, Halverson's department isn't done with it. After completing work on, for example, Ronon's new jacket for the fourth season, the designer handed it over to her "breakdown artist", Charis Tilson, to perform yet more magic.

"Usually what we're trying to do is make a costume look more worn, lived in, used," Halverson explains of the process. "So for that she'll just sand it — if it's a dark costume she'll maybe bring some paint onto it to make it look worn or soiled in some way. If it's a light costume you put dark on, if it's a dark costume you put light on. She uses waxes, oils, paints and sanding, things like that. We've had really specific episodes, like 'Travelers', which was a rusted bucket of a ship, where we actually took the costume and rusted it down using special gel paints that had tints in them, and it was one of my favorite episodes. We also did one called 'Missing', which has the Bola Kai in it, who were essentially cave men. We built all these costumes that were brand new, but our director Andy Mikita had made a passing comment that, 'Wouldn't it be great if these guys disappeared into the woods?' Someone passed on that little tidbit to me, so we developed a technique of using rubber and creating a bark effect. We put those on their breastplates and wove them into their pants. So in fact there was one scene where he had them in the forest, and they did kind of disappear. He didn't know we were doing it, so it was a really pleasant surprise for him.

"We're always looking for a new thing to do," Halverson says with another bright smile. "It's always fun!" Å

Above: The Bola Kai had particularly detailed 'camouflage' costumes.

CONSTRUCTION

SCOTT WELLENBRINK

Scott Wellenbrink has been working in the set construction business for just over ten years — ever since he visited his wife, who worked at Bridge Studios on a show called *Stargate SG-1*, in fact… "I've worked in many different jobs," says Wellenbrink. "But my wife, she worked on *MacGyver*, so she was offered a job on *Stargate SG-1*. And when I came to visit I thought, '*This* is what I should be doing — this is just too much fun!'" He laughs, recalling the revelation that would change his working life forever. "I was the guy that tinkered with motorcycles — I still do — making something out of nothing all the time. And all of a sudden I was around all these people that I had so much in common with. I think that when you're really passionate about something you just can't help it — you just want to be there, you just want to *do* it. So I went in to the boss, Tom Wells, and said that I didn't know anything about what he did but that I wanted to work here. A couple of days later my phone rang and that was it! I like it here. I've been here so long now that it feels like home. They're great people to work for — you have a problem and they'll help you fix it. They never just give you the bad news. They always try to work it out with you."

Over his years on *Stargate SG-1* and various other film projects, Wellenbrink turned that enthusiasm into skill, and now operates as the *Stargate: Atlantis* construction coordinator. Between Wellenbrink and his team of set builders, carpenters and painters, the construction department repeatedly makes 'something out of nothing' — for it is their job to take production designer James Robbins' beautiful concept drawings and turn them into the sets you see every week.

"It's always exciting," says Wellenbrink. "I see the concept before I see the words, because I work directly with James Robbins. So we're usually talking about what sets are required before I even read the script. Within a day or two I'll read

Below: A twenty-foot exterior wall section of Atlantis's tower was built for 'Quarantine'.

Above: Season four called
for a revised Wraith set.

the script and find out within what context we're going to put the set. But I get excited
— there's the normal hallway stuff that can become a little dry, but whenever you're
building a new set, whatever it is, whether it's a simple room or something else, I
always like to see it from beginning to end. I'd have to say that some are more exciting
than others, but generally I just like them all. You start with an idea and that blossoms
into a drawing, and as soon as we're inside James Robbins' brain with what he's trying
to build, from that point it's simple for us. We just need to know what he's thinking
and we can give him ideas and maybe ask for changes."

Some sets are of course more difficult than others. *Stargate: Atlantis* has several
'standing sets' that are major undertakings — large, fixed structures such as the village
set, the Wraith set and the gateroom set that are all designed to be reused over and
over. Then there are other, smaller and more temporary sets that will be built for
specific episodes.

The standing sets are built before production begins or, as in the case of the village,
between seasons, and require far more work than the changeable episodic sets.
Standing sets are more solid, are often built on more than one level, and therefore
have to accommodate more weight. This will require significant infrastructure, such
as solid construction pipes, which constitute the 'bones' of the set. Around this
infrastructure will be built the external features seen by audiences around the world.
Building such a structure takes a lot of time, manpower and money, hence it's not

CONSTRUCTION

Above: One of the show's most photographed 'standing sets'.

Opposite: An amazing set from 'Trio'.

something that can be done while filming of the season is in process.

"There are a lot of factors involved in getting to the end result," says Wellenbrink, "and the number one thing I look at is the time. If you have six months or four months to build a set and any amount of money, you can do just about anything. The guys that we work with are incredibly talented. In talking about the village, we knew when it had to shoot and we worked back from that. James comes up with a concept as per what's written. He designs what he thinks the village should look like and passes that by the writers and they agree or disagree and make changes. And they see roughly what it will cost. The amount of time I have is directly reflected in the price of the set. If you're going to run at it with a whole bunch of guys in a short amount of time, you're going to eat the money up quite quickly. So I'll work that out backwards: when I have to be finished and how many people I think are going to be required to paint it and everything."

Smaller, more temporary sets are entirely different, though naturally they still require time and money. It's these that Wellenbrink's team will spend most of their energy constructing throughout the year — smaller plywood structures, sometimes built inside larger sets, that must look solid enough to keep the audience in the story and accommodate the needs of the shooting crew.

"In a standalone set, we're building a small box inside a bigger box, the studio. At that point there's things you need to protect, like your height, width and doorways, machine access and things like that. Most of it is built back at our shop, and put on trucks or on trailers and assembled on site. So it's not like building a house at all where you can just get in the studio and when you're done you're done. Everything needs to come apart and get recycled, shot again as something else, or components [of something else] — fancy doors or windows get slightly altered and reused to save money and time. Everything needs to be 'wild', which means removable for camera access. You're that person outside the building looking at the people inside. You put the viewer behind the wall, so the wall has to come away and it just gives it more room to act and for access. I don't know how they act in a room where there's things missing!"

CONSTRUCTION

The latter half of season four benefited from the sets that had been created for *Stargate: Continuum*, the movie that had been shooting at the studio earlier in the year. With those extra sets already in place — also built by Wellenbrink and his team — *Stargate: Atlantis* could take advantage of these new environments. Martin Gero decided to use the set that had been constructed for the ship scenes in *Continuum* to create the basis for the story in 'Trio', for example. Rather than requiring the construction department to build an entirely new set, the script called for the set to be turned into something new. The advantage of this particular set was that it had been built on a gimble — a hydraulic system that meant the set could be tilted. This is not something that could have been accomplished on *Stargate: Atlantis*'s normal construction budget.

"It was very involved," Wellenbrink recalls, "with the underground bunker set as well as the big climbing wall that we built. Both were a good size for the show. It was a neat script and there were a lot of things to overcome there, with the planks and the various gags. So it was kind of fun to work all that out. They took advantage of the set being on the gimble, which is a device that allows the set to be tipped in one direction, and they wanted to tip it a little further and design it like the underground bunker was giving way and they had to find a way back out through the top. It's a lot of fun building those kinds of things. You've got to think outside the norm."

Another of Wellenbrink's favorite sets from season four was constructed for 'Travelers'.

"A lot of that set was [dressed with] hoses and wires," he says. "It was the texture that worked so well with the camera. It's so busy — the feeling is clutter and age, and it's just different. Everybody gets used to the pristine, polished look, but I think people find age quite refreshing at times, to see something with that kind of scope. The 'Travelers' set wasn't a complicated build, it was two big rooms and a long connective corridor. For the shape, once you build one of the arches, you're just mass-producing them, so that set wasn't a particularly tricky one. But the paint finish on that one was terrific."

Once the basic construction on a set is finished, it's the painters and set decorators that really finish the piece off, giving a set the texture and detail that completes the look.

"Steve Craine and his gang are tremendous," Wellenbrink notes. "I always think that the set is a set and that's fine — it's just wood and plywood. But once the painters go through, it really gets the depth. The trick is knowing when to stop. You can make it go too far over the top."

With a set ready to go and approved by Robbins and the producers, Wellenbrink's job is almost done. However, he does need to be on hand during a shoot to keep an eye on anything that might need doing, because the production's need to re-use each set as much as possible can require the coordinator's attention.

Above: The 'Travelers' set was one of Wellenbrink's favorites.

"There are things called changeovers, where we'll play a single room as two different rooms," he explains. "You play the same set as two different but similar sets. So we'll have to change out a ceiling or a wall or just do an overnight changeover where things leave and come in differently. That's often more to do with set decoration, and is a bit simpler. That's the magic of film, you never really know where you are because you can't relate it to where you've just been! The cameraman will put his back to the wall and you have no idea what's behind you."

Wellenbrink and his team have worked with the production for so long that it's rare that any significant, unexpected alterations to the set are needed. With everyone working together, each department is on the same page — but that doesn't mean that construction is averse to changing something at the last minute if required.

"The directors and the DoPs [directors of photography] are very involved in the process," Wellenbrink says, "and early on we'll ask them what they want and any special requirements such as camera positions or this or that, and we'll build and allow for that. They're pretty good, they'll stick to that for the most part, but there's always things that evolve and I'm all for evolution! I just love to make it work and if everybody's happy, I'll be the first one to make changes on the day or at the last minute. I think that's just fine. It's all for the betterment of the look, so let's do it!" Å

CASTING

PAUL WEBER

P aul Weber has been *Stargate: Atlantis*'s Los Angeles-based casting director since the show began, and before that he also worked on *Stargate SG-1*. The series also has a casting director in Vancouver, and between them, they are responsible for peopling the whole *Stargate* universe.

Casting, whether for a movie or a television series, is a tremendous skill. It requires a casting director to find the perfect actor for a specific role without any of the attendant elements that create the finished product — in the audition room there are no sets, no costumes, no other actors to react against, and sometimes not even a complete script. It's challenging enough for a drama series with its roots firmly on Earth. Casting for a series set in another galaxy is a whole other kettle of fish.

"This kind of genre is very specific and very challenging in terms of casting," says Weber. "You've got very smart writing, intricate storylines, and very challenging dialogue. No one really gets off easy in this show in terms of guest stars! If you're an Earth- or base-bound character, you will likely need to be able to handle intricate technical language. If you are an off-world character, you need to have a facility with language that is almost mythical in it's nature because of the kind of language that the writers use. It's language that actors need to be able to wrap themselves around — they need to be able to compete with the scenery without chewing it too badly!"

To find actors that can cope with these demands, Weber says that he often turns to stage-trained performers. "They know how to handle the kind of language that this genre requires," the casting director explains. "You also have to add the emotional and physical demands that these roles make, too. We ask a *lot* from the guest leads that audition for the show, and a lot of American actors, although very good, don't always understand the tone or scale of the show. *Stargate: Atlantis* is a little different from the *CSI*-style of acting, which is minimalist and precise. We paint on a larger canvas, and we need actors that can paint with bold colors."

Weber has been working with the *Stargate* producers for so long that he largely knows what they want in a role. He'll get a heads-up, usually before the script is done, and will go to work arranging auditions for thirty to forty actors.

"They are relatively short conversations because we understand each other," says Weber. "We can refer back to a certain actor or a certain type of role that we've done in the past, and use that as a prototype. After a brief conversation, even if the script isn't written, I'll know what the guys are looking for. It's terrific because they have scripts ready often two to three weeks in advance. There are many shows that are written just days before shooting, or they'll have a script that's not even written until

Above: Casting a show like *Stargate: Atlantis* takes special skill.

the night before. That's really difficult. But these guys tend to map out story arcs in advance and they deliver scripts early, which makes my job much easier."

Weber has a plethora of sources to draw from — including other shows that place similar demands on the actors.

"Sometimes we look at other genre shows," he explains. "It helps ratings for us, and it also makes us feel comfortable that we have the kind of actor that we know is familiar with the genre — like Robert Picardo or Connor Trinneer. Actors like that we feel comfortable with, because they have come from another genre series, and they understand it."

Weber films each audition, and after narrowing the selection further, sends digital files of the recordings to the production offices for the producers to make their choices. The field is usually narrowed down to three or four actors. It's then down to Weber to make an offer, finding who is available in the slots required. "If our first choice is available and we cast them, terrific," he says. "Our second and third choices we save for another episode."

Sometimes, of course, the production goes with 'stunt' casting — writing an episode for a specific actor known to the audience. "That comes up relatively often, where the guys have someone in mind and I will try to go after that actor. And if they are available and interested, we will book them, because the show is a great kick for a lot of actors to do who don't normally get to do sci-fi. There's an actor from *E.R.*, Goran Visnjic, who is a big fan of the show. We keep trying to find something for him!" Å

STAND-INS

LEBRONE WADE

Stand-ins are another vital but generally unsung group of people that work behind the scenes to put an episode of *Stargate: Atlantis* together. Ever-present during filming, they rarely get much visible time on screen, and yet without them there to step in whenever needed, the cast and crew's job would take on a further layer of complication.

Lebrone Wade is tall, broad shouldered, and spends most of his time carrying around a large hairy object that he has nicknamed "Precious". Wade is Jason Momoa's stand-in, and Precious is the wig he wears to more closely resemble Ronon Dex, since Wade himself has very short hair. When he's not wearing Precious, the knots of hair appear to have become something of a pet. But then, long hours on a film set can often addle the brain...

Wade is just one of the main cast's dedicated stand-in crew. Each of the regular characters has their own — Gerry Durand stands in for Joe Flanigan as Sheppard, Ashley O'Connell shadows Rachel Luttrell, and Chuck Campbell, whom regular viewers will recognize as Chuck the gateroom technician, stands in for David Hewlett.

"Basically, a stand-in is the person that assists the whole crew in setting up the shot," Wade explains. "The cast will come in and they will block and rehearse the scene, and then the stand-ins will come in and run the scene over and over again, just to make sure that the whole set-up is perfect — that the lighting is correct, that everything on the set is as it should be. So that when the actor does come in, everything is set up and they just need to execute the shot."

The set up process for each shot can take a long time — each department that forms the shooting crew, from the director right through to lighting, sound and the camera operator, needs time to make sure that their equipment is correctly adjusted to where the actor will be when the camera begins to roll. Having stand-ins to mimic the action of the scene to be shot means that the main cast do not have to be present during this set up period.

It's important that a stand-in resembles the actor they are replacing, if not in facial features then other physical ways. In actual fact, some stand-ins do bear a striking similarity to the main cast, and though without the wig and costume Wade is easy to tell apart from Jason Momoa, it was for his close match to the actor that he was originally chosen.

"I actually started off as his photo double," Wade recalls. "Actors sometimes have scheduling conflicts and they just need someone to step in and do the work for them when the crew need insert shots or shots of body parts — over the shoulder type things. Him and I have the same skin tone, the same body type and the same proportions. So

my agent called me up and said, 'Hey, do you want to come and double for him?' So I did that a couple of times and then when season four came around, they needed a stand-in for him, and they called me up and asked if I wanted the job."

For instances when he is actually photo doubling, Precious — a poor approximation of Ronon's mass of dreadlocks, it has to be said — is replaced by Momoa's actual wig, and the look is completed with the actor's real wardrobe. The finishing touch is a smattering of matching facial hair, applied by the make-up department, and Wade says that when he's in the full getup, the resemblance can be quite spooky.

"I definitely don't look exactly like him, but actually when I'm doubling for him and I have the goatee and the wig on, then it's surprisingly close. People will come up and talk to me like I'm Jason. And then you can see it in their face — they'll be halfway through a sentence and they'll trail off and go, 'Oh! You're not Jason…'" he laughs.

Even without the photo doubling aspect of his job, the fact that Wade is such a match for the actor he's standing in for is a massive help to the production. To be able to accurately set up a shot around the 'second team', as the group of stand-ins are collectively called, they have to give the crew as close an approximation to the main cast as possible.

"When you're trying to set up a shot, if there's someone that's five foot three standing in for someone that's six foot four and it's a close-up head shot, it's not

Above: David Hewlett's stand-in, Chuck Campbell, also has a role as Chuck the gateroom technician.

necessarily going to work. Someone that's five foot three, their head isn't going to be in the right spot. If you're trying to get a perfect shot of the actor, you need someone who looks somewhat like the actor just so that they represent them in the best possible way."

Matching skin tone is also important, since the lighting department needs to know exactly how an environment is going to play visually once the first team are back in position and ready for a take. And, obviously, Ronon is a very physical character, and though Wade would not be called in to double for Momoa in a full-on stunt, he has found himself sparring now and then.

"There's a scene that I did a couple of weeks ago, a big sword fight, and I was doubling for him," he says. "So you couldn't actually see me, but it was a shot that they needed for the episode that they didn't actually shoot on the day. What happens is that sometimes they'll have all the episode done and they'll realize that, 'Well, this would look good if we had a certain shot just to complete the scene.' This was basically just a silhouette of him fighting with another character and in the background there was Sheppard firing off his gun. But Jason was busy, so they called me in and dressed me up like him and put his wig on me and I did some sword fighting!"

Below: A shot such as this requires a double skilled in stunts.

Wade obviously enjoys his position on the *Stargate: Atlantis* set, though it entails a lot of waiting for something to happen.

"It's a pretty full-time job," Wade explains. "Basically whenever Jason's here, I'm here. So I'm here to assist the crew and assist him. I'll help set up the shot and run the scenes when they need to. Sometimes I'll help him out too, I'll run lines with him. It's a great crew, a great place to be working. You hear stories from other shows about people screaming at each other and things of that nature, but none of that happens here. None of us mind coming to work, and we all have a good time. It's a good show."

Being a stand-in generally isn't a career choice — as with many jobs on a film set, people get into them through circuitous routes. Wade started out as a model and actor, but says he appreciates the regular nature of the work. For the moment, he's happy to continue as he is, and has committed himself to doing the best job he can for the cast and crew of *Stargate: Atlantis*.

Above: Lebrone Wade is Jason Momoa's stand-in and double.

"My availability has become somewhat limited just because I am here. If there is anything that the ADs [assistant directors] can do to let me off so I can go and pursue acting or modeling and photography then they will do the best that they can. There's a reason that I'm here though, and as of right now, this is my priority, so I have to make sure that I'm here and that everything is taken care of."

In fact, being Jason Momoa's stand-in doesn't preclude Wade from appearing in the show as another character. It's something that often happens for stand-ins that have been with a production for a long time, particularly one such as *Stargate: Atlantis*, which has a high volume of background characters. Take Chuck Campbell, for example, who regularly has speaking parts. Gerry Durand, too, who has been with the show since the first season, can often be glimpsed on screen, and in 'Adrift' he played a named character, Captain Levine.

"A lot of other stand-ins have characters on the show," Wade points out. "I'm the newest, so they haven't given me a character yet. But maybe, if I'm lucky!" Å

ON-SET SOUND

PATRICK RAMSAY

One of the many departments that make up part of the shooting crew on any *Stargate: Atlantis* episode is on-set sound. Patrick Ramsay is the production's on-set sound mixer, and can most often be found behind his small bank of monitors, flanked by two iBooks, one of which is likely to be playing some of his eclectic music collection between set ups. Ramsay's team also comprises Dave Griffiths, the boom operator, and Naan Spiess, their technical assistant.

Recording sound on a film is a tricky but absolutely vital business. It's easy to forget when watching a finished episode that everything on the screen has been created deliberately. That goes for the sound as well — and not just the effects and music, but the basic ambiance of where our characters are and what they are saying. When a camera rolls, it doesn't record those things, and even if it did all you would get is a blur of unmetered, unregulated background sound. Ramsay's team's job is to make sure that the vital sounds on set are recorded at the right levels — the actor's lines, the atmosphere of the room. They capture as much of the actor's performance as possible, at as high a quality as possible, so that the sound recorded on the day can be used in the final cut. It's a big job for three people, and it's important that the sound remains as consistent as possible for the editor to use in post-production.

"We have a variety of different microphones that we use, and because we use different cameras, sometimes three or four, we have wireless mics on each of the actors as well as the overhead microphones, and so each of those microphones goes to its own track on a multi-track recorder," Ramsay explains. "Then I do an actual mix of all the dialogue each time we roll. So there's a mono mix, which is a single track, plus a mix of all the actors' microphones, and it sounds as if it's all coming from one microphone, as if one microphone was getting everything. So from each angle that we do, I try to match it, so that whether we're in a wide shot or a tight shot, I'm giving the editor a mixed track so that the dialogue always sounds the same for each character."

Mixing in this fashion means that Ramsay is controlling the levels for each track running into the computer. This allows for a more consistent soundtrack for the editor to work with, and means less work in post-production to get the levels right. For example, if there's a scene in which McKay and Zelenka are having an argument (or in fact McKay and *anyone* are having an argument!), it's Ramsay's job to make sure that each of the voices can be heard clearly, and aren't 'spiking', in other words rising so high that the sound is distorted. And if there's a noisy prop or piece of action going on adjacent to the dialogue, the sound mixer must make sure that it's the dialogue

heard first and foremost, not the background noise.

"When you watch in English, almost everything that you hear in terms of dialogue is what I have recorded on set," Ramsay explains. "I have Dave and Naan working with me. Dave has been my boom operator for about ten years and Naan's been our sound assistant for six years. We each have our own responsibilities. So Naan will make sure that each of the actors has got a wireless microphone on, and things like if we have big, clompy feet we'll lay carpets so that you can hear what they're saying instead of the noise of their feet."

The wireless microphone tech packs are about five by three by one inches, small enough to be concealed beneath an actor's clothing, with the microphone itself tucked into clothing closer to the mouth. The *Atlantis* regulars usually wear theirs strapped to their legs, beneath their uniforms. Although this ensures that Ramsay can record all of the actor's dialogue cleanly, it's not his favorite way of getting a good sound.

"Dave will be on set making sure that whatever shots he can he'll get on the boom, which is the overhead microphone," the sound mixer explains, "because it always sounds better than a wireless microphone. The perspective is always right, and you get to hear the room around the voice. You also get a sense of the room that they're in, and quite often when we're mixing I'll have the overhead microphone as well as part of the track, maybe not getting the whole voice but part of it. Then they've got the personal microphone and also the overhead microphone, so it's not just that really dry sound that you would get from a wireless microphone. Then, if we're doing shots where we're doing a wide shot showing everybody as well as close-ups, in the final mix — which they will do on the mixing stage where they've got a hundred tracks running effects and everything else — they will be able to take my mixed tracks and maybe take that close-up sound. And if they need to move it into a wide shot, they will add a bit of extra 'room' sound to it to open it up and make it sound the correct perspective."

The sound department's first task during a day of filming various scenes is to work out where the director is going to move and what sort of environment they will be recording in. "Before we start any scene, we always do a blocking," Ramsay explains. "That's where everyone gets to come in and watch. Generally what we'll do is a private blocking where it's just the director, the continuity supervisor, the director of photography and someone from the sound department. The blocking is where the scene evolves, the actors decide where they want to move to and they block out where the camera will go. Then everyone gets to come in after they've worked that out and we do a public blocking where everyone can see exactly what's going to happen. Sometimes we'll make some comments — if, for example, there's a camera that will

Below: Actor David Nykl crawls through a plywood vent — the clanging sound effects are added later to allow greater sound control.

make it impossible for us to get the sound we need, we'll change the camera, or maybe not run one camera during a shot. Generally before we shoot we know exactly what we're going to do. You have to work with everyone all the time, so there can be a prop that's noisy or there can be fans from special effects that can be noisy. In the sound department you're always reacting to things. Something will come up and you have to fix it as you go, so you have to be really on your toes and anticipate what can go wrong."

This is particularly the case

in situations where the production is outside the studio, on location. Inside the studio, though there is still noise everywhere, it is to a certain extent controllable. Everyone knows that when the assistant directors yell "Rolling" and the lights outside the set start flashing, extraneous sound will stop. People stop talking, stop moving. But outside, it's far more difficult. There is traffic, wind, dogs barking, alarms going off… you name it, it's there.

"Out on location is more difficult a lot of the time," agrees Ramsay. "It can be a blessing and a curse. You can be in beautiful environments where it just sounds amazing. Or you can be in noisy environments where you have to use the wireless microphones a lot, and you just do the best that you can. You equalize and you try to get the closest perspective on the actor. Sometimes you'll ask them, with certain lines, to speak up a bit, and you have to be careful. You may have an actor that is trying to act but their voice will disappear. So you say to them, 'Well, either you can do this all later in ADR [additional dialogue recording], or if you just bring it up a notch, I'll be able to get it. You have to be careful with that — you don't want to destroy their performance, and you don't want to get between the actor and the director.

"But location is great in many ways," he continues, "because you can do great sound effects when you are there. We can run separate microphones a hundred feet away, to get the background sound to get the birds in the trees. You can get a wonderful ambiance so that when they do the final mix, you really get a sense of where you are." Å

Above: Each actor has a personal microphone, concealed beneath their costumes.

JENNIFER JOHNSON

I n many ways, for the television viewer post-production is the most ephemeral of the processes an episode goes through on its way to the screen. The more obvious aspects of production to talk about are the writing, the directing and the acting that go into making a show so great. But post-production is where the huge jigsaw puzzle that is an episode of *Stargate: Atlantis* comes together, and Jennifer Johnson is the person that guides it right the way through.

The post-production offices are a long, thin line of rooms that back onto the *Stargate: Atlantis* effects stage, which houses the huge village set and the Ancient chair set, amongst others. Johnson's office is so close to the action, in fact, that the alarm bell that goes off to alert people that the camera is rolling can be heard from her office.

"I'm the associate producer," Johnson says, "so basically, I start right at the beginning and we set out what the post schedule for the year is going to be. And when the footage is shot I am the go-between between film and production."

Johnson's job is varied and starts as soon as a script first arrives from a writer. Attending all the production meetings, even before production begins, allows her to judge what special needs a particular episode might have besides the usual post processes of editing, sound design and additional dialogue recording (ADR).

"Our input there is to look for things that relate to post in terms of stock footage, sourcing music — things that are written into the script that we will be responsible for," she elaborates. "So, for example, when you see 'stock shot' written in a scene, I have a production coordinator that goes through this whole bevy of resources that we have, pulling in the stock footage and showing them to the producers to see what shot they like. Then we're responsible for licensing and getting clearances for all of that. Sometimes there will be reuses of shots from previous episodes, such as visual effects, and it's our responsibility to try to find that and give it to the director and producers before they go to camera. Right now we've got a 'clip show', so I'm dealing with that. The writer writes out what they want to see for the clip. We read the script and then the assistant editors pull together those old shows and put those clips together. We'll have a reel and then the editor, as they're working on the show, will drop the pieces in and re-work the scene."

Once an episode goes into production and in front of the camera, Johnson is the one who deals with any issues that may crop up. In years gone by, when everything was shot on physical film, the daily reels would be sent to a laboratory overnight to be processed so that the director and producers could review footage the next day. The associate producer would be the first port of call if something awry was noticed during this process. There was a lot that could go wrong, either as a result of what

had happened on set during filming or because of accidents during processing. Now, with the advent of HD video, things are a little different — though that doesn't necessarily make it all plain sailing for the associate producer.

"I can get calls at any time during the night saying there's this problem or that problem. We run that through and see whether we are covered — is everything all right? And then I call production and say, 'We have this problem, but here are our options.' We have such a great crew and very rarely do things go wrong," says Johnson. "It's just weird technical issues with the camera — but they're different now. The problems used to be dirt and scratches and hairs, and now it's pixels. And our process is so completely different to how it was a year ago with season three. We do quite a bit here on the lot. "

Once the episode is 'in the can', post-production really kicks into gear. Most of the department's space is taken up by a row of small editing suites, which is where an episode begins to take shape. Working with the script, each editor will begin cutting the show together in Final Cut Pro as soon as the dailies are okayed by the producers. Though Johnson oversees this aspect of the process too, she's quick to stress that it's really a case of leaving the editors to do what they are best at. "It's an artistic job, so I'm just here to help them if they need anything," she says. "We have some great

Above: This scene, shot on location, is one that could possibly require additional dialogue recording (ADR).

editors and they're really talented. The show is shot typically for seven days. What will happen is, when a show has finished shooting, our editor gets a day to complete his assembly. Then the director comes in for a few days, the producers come in for two days and then it goes to the network.

Once editing is completed and signed off by the director, producers and network, an episode is termed as 'locked', which means that from that point on, the content and sequence of scenes will not change. "So typically from the end of shooting to the lock is about two weeks," Johnson continues. "That's just for the editing."

Stargate: Atlantis is a visual effects-driven show, and within that locked edit will be all the timed space that visual effects supervisor Mark Savela needs to drop in those spectacular sequences. Of course, they don't go into the edit fully-formed, since the intricate effects sequences are the last parts of an episode to be finalized. But Johnson's next job is supervising the creation of the sound effects that will go with the episode's final mix soundtrack, so she needs something to work to.

Below: Scenes such as this have the potential for problems that need to be 'fixed in post'.

"It really is driven by visual effects," she reiterates. "From the locked point the next thing we have is the first vfx output, which is 'temps'. That drives what becomes my job, which is sound. So we'll get the temporary visual effects to our sound designer and talk about it and get input from producers about what they want to hear."

Working on sound effects isn't the only thing that happens during this period — the soundscape as a whole is Johnson's responsibility, and this is when she decides, along with Sharp Sound, *Stargate: Atlantis*'s sound facility, what parts of the show need to go through additional dialogue recording. ADR is a vital part of post-production. Though the production tries to record as much sound on set during filming as possible, sometimes it's necessary to pick up lines that have dropped out.

"A lot of times they're shooting on location and they're supposed to be on another planet in another galaxy but there are airplanes, or construction, or traffic," Johnson says ruefully. "It's all things that don't really help sell that

Above: The team, as we know them best.

you're on another planet! So basically, I'm looking for technical issues. It's mostly for weird background sounds. Sometimes it's line replacements, where the producers want to hear a different line or an added line. We try to stay away as much as possible from ADR just because it's great to keep the original performance."

ADR is also a strange experience for the actors, who must go into a sound booth and watch a recording of the original line that needs replacing. The task is then to deliver the line again, as closely as they can to their original performance, so that the sound editor can drop it in as seamlessly as possible.

"So," Johnson explains, "from the time we see temporary visual effects, it's typically three weeks to a month before we see the first finals and then about a week later I do my day-one mix, which is such an incredibly long, busy day!"

This mix is when all the various elements of sound come together beside the visual edited episode. It's an incredible skill to weave in so many tracks to so much action — sound effects, dialogue, music and so on.

"The producers watch that and then give notes, and then we wait for the visual effects to be finalized. Once that happens, that's when post completes. We typically have about two weeks after the final visual effects, which is where our job really comes into it — completing the mix, color timing, titling it… all our different deliverables."

So, the next time you sit down to watch an episode, spare a thought for Jennifer Johnson and her team! Å

p156, top: Atlantis finds its new home, in 'Lifeline'.
p156, bottom: The *Daedalus* and the *Apollo* arrive to help, in 'Be All My Sins Remember'd'.
p157, top: The attack on the Replicator homeworld.
p157, bottom: One last surprise for the audience.

VISUAL EFFECTS

BIG FINISH

THE GATE IS STILL OPEN
THE MISSIONS CONTINUE

STARGATE
SG·1™

STARGATE
ATLANTIS™

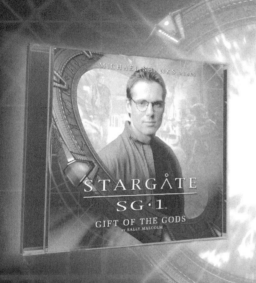

ALL-NEW AUDIO ADVENTURES ON CD

SIX NEW STORIES READ BY THE ORIGINAL CAST

• FULL DRAMATIC READING
• CINEMATIC SOUND DESIGN
• SPECIALLY COMPOSED MUSICAL SCORE
• EXCLUSIVE BONUS AUDIO INTERVIEWS

AVAILABLE FROM ALL GOOD BOOKSHOPS OR BUY DIRECT FROM BIG FINISH

WWW.BIGFINISH.COM
CREDIT CARD HOTLINE: TEL 01628 824102
FREE UK DELIVERY ON EVERYTHING